12 TOOLS FOR LEARNING SPANISH

POWER TOOLS, HAND TOOLS, NUTS & BOLTS

MARK RHEA

12 Tools For Learning Spanish

Copyright © 2010 by Mark Rhea

ISBN-10 0615420966
ISBN-13 9780615420967

Printed in USA by 48HrBooks (www.48HrBooks.com)

Designed by Andrew Little
Edited by Melissa Salazar

Endless thanks to my wife Becky, and daughters Opal and Bessma, for their support and inspiration. Also, I would like to thank my first and best Spanish teacher, Warren Hardy in San Miguel de Allende (warrenhardy.com). Warren's guidance and friendship over the last 20 years have been enormously important in my own career.

Thank you,
Mark

Contents

INTRODUCTION

How To Use This Book — Page 1

BEFORE GETTING STARTED — Page 2
Verbs: The Key To Communication
Personal Pronouns
Using Courtesies: Saying Hello & Goodbye

SPOKEN SECTIONS & CHAPTERS

POWER TOOLS — SECTION 1
Chapter 1   Needs & Wants: Fast Verbs — Page 7
Chapter 2   The Future: Ir+a+infinitive — Page 17
Chapter 3   Likes & Dislikes: Gustar — Page 23
Chapter 4   Expressing Obligation: Tener+que+infinitive — Page 30

HAND TOOLS — SECTION 2
Chapter 5   Identifying Origin, Characteristics, Occupation & Relationships: Ser — Page 39
Chapter 6   Describing Condition & Telling Location: Estar — Page 44
Chapter 7   People & Things: Object Pronouns — Page 50
Chapter 8   There Is / There Are: Hay — Page 61

NUTS & BOLTS — SECTION 3
Chapter 9   Instruction & Suggestion: Commands — Page 67
Chapter 10 Reflexive Verbs — Page 74
Chapter 11 To Know: Saber & Conocer — Page 78
Chapter 12 Past Tenses: Preterite & Imperfect — Page 81

REFERENCE SECTIONS & CHAPTERS

THE TOOL SHED — SECTION 4
Chapter 13 The Essential Tenses — Page 91
Chapter 14 Asking Questions: Interrogatives — Page 102
Chapter 15 Key Irregular Verbs — Page 104
Chapter 16 Pronunciation — Page 107

Contents

Chapter 17 Making Words Match   Page 111
Chapter 18 Possession   Page 117
Chapter 19 Telling Time   Page 121
Chapter 20 Demonstrative Adjectives & Pronouns   Page 129
Chapter 21 Comparisons   Page 130
Chapter 22 Contractions   Page 131
Chapter 23 Stem-Changing Verbs   Page 132
Chapter 24 Por & Para   Page 133
Chapter 25 Present Progressive   Page 135
Chapter 26 Numbers   Page 137

VOCABULARY   **SECTION 5**
Chapter 27 Taking a Trip and Lodging   Page 140
Chapter 28 Getting Around Roads & Cities   Page 142
Chapter 29 Restaurant & Food   Page 144
Chapter 30 Family & Home   Page 146
Chapter 31 Daily Routine   Page 148
Chapter 32 Sports & Games   Page 150
Chapter 33 Art & Culture   Page 152
Chapter 34 Health & Medicine   Page 153
Chapter 35 Social Life   Page 155
Chapter 36 Politics & The Media   Page 157
Chapter 37 Work & Professions   Page 159
Chapter 38 School   Page 161
Chapter 39 Clothes   Page 163
Chapter 40 Essential Words   Page 165
Chapter 41 Most Common Verbs   Page 167
Chapter 42 Instant Vocabulary: Cognates   Page 169
Chapter 43 Adjectives   Page 171

GLOSSARY OF TERMS   **PAGE 173**

Introduction

HOW TO USE THIS BOOK

12 Tools for Learning Spanish breaks the mold by organizing language into specific tasks, giving the student the tools to communicate effectively right from the start. Unlike traditional language books that present lessons from the easiest to the most difficult, **12 Tools for Learning Spanish** emphasizes what Spanish speakers use most.

Like any good toolbox, **12 Tools for Learning Spanish** gives the language student the right tool for the task, minimizing the fluff and filler found in most textbooks and phrase books. **12 Tools for Learning Spanish** is divided into two broad categories: speaking sections (**Power Tools, Hand Tools,** and **Nuts & Bolts**), and a comprehensive reference section (**The Tool Shed**) for even the most advanced student.

IF YOU STUDIED SPANISH IN HIGH SCHOOL OR COLLEGE

This book was written with you in mind! Begin with Chapter 1 and work your way down the Table of Contents. The spoken sections (**Power Tools, Hand Tools, Nuts and Bolts**) highlight the most important and basic uses of Spanish. These sections clarify what you have previously studied and are organized to move you towards speaking Spanish. After mastering the **Power Tools, Hand Tools, Nuts & Bolts,** continue on to the reference sections (**The Tool Shed**) to further perfect your skills.

THE COMPLETE BEGINNER

If you have never been exposed to Spanish, use the alternatively-ordered Table of Contents below. Start with Chapter 16 and make your way down the list. Focus on the information you find most useful, moving quickly as needed. Don't waste time!

Chapter 16	Pronunciation	Page 107
Chapter 17	Making Words Match	Page 111
Chapter 42	Instant Vocabulary: Cognates	Page 169
Chapter 40	Essential Words	Page 165
Chapters 27 – 43	Vocabulary	Page 140
Chapter 41	Most Common Verbs	Page 167
Chapters 1 – 4	Power Tools	Page 7
Chapters 5 – 8	Hand Tools	Page 39
Chapters 9 – 12	Nuts & Bolts	Page 67

Introduction

THE ADVANCED STUDENT

If you have experience speaking Spanish, review **Chapter 13, The Essential Tenses,** for an explanation of all present, past, and future tenses. Once **The Essential Tenses** are mastered, review the Table of Contents for other sections of interest.

BEFORE GETTING STARTED

The spoken sections and chapters are divided into three parts: **Power Tools, Hand Tools,** and **Nuts & Bolts.** The most important and practical section is **Power Tools,** followed by **Hand Tools,** and finally, **Nuts & Bolts.** The reference sections and chapters include **The Tool Shed,** and **Vocabulary** sections.

> **Power Tools** focuses on how to communicate basic *wants, desires, future plans, likes & dislikes,* and *needs.*
>
> **Hand Tools** is essential for describing and identifying your surroundings and yourself.
>
> **Nuts & Bolts** covers common structures like commands and past tenses.
>
> **The Tool Shed** is a comprehensive reference and review for every level, from beginning to advanced. It includes a review of every important tense and construction as well as telling time, possession, irregular verb charts, and more.
>
> **Vocabulary** consists of 13 theme-based vocabulary sections, the essential "fill-in" words, common verbs, cognates (words that are similar in Spanish and English), and adjectives.

To get started, let's review some basic information like verbs, personal pronouns, and common courtesies.

Verbs: The Key To Communication

Verbs[1] are essential for both speaking and understanding language, and help to communicate the "big picture" by telling us *what is happening.* Below is a quick overview of how verbs change in English and Spanish, and some of the words used to describe verbs.

In English, verbs do not **change,** or **conjugate,** often. We either say *live,* or *lives*: I, you, we, they, or you all *live,* or, he or she *lives.* In Spanish, however, the verb *to live* has five different forms! Look at the comparison of *to live* in English and Spanish (**vivir**) on the next page.

---

[1] Verbs are "action words" and tell us who is doing what. In the sentence, *John bakes cookies, bakes* is the verb and tells what is happening in the sentence.

Introduction

The form of the verb in bold (To Live, Vivir), is called the INFINITIVE. The forms listed below the INFINITIVE are called CONJUGATIONS.

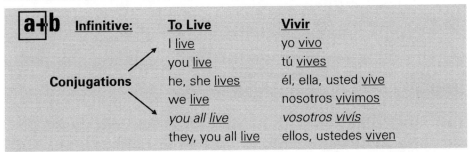

a+b Infinitive:	**To Live**	**Vivir**
	I <u>live</u>	yo <u>vivo</u>
	you <u>live</u>	tú <u>vives</u>
Conjugations	he, she <u>lives</u>	él, ella, usted <u>vive</u>
	we <u>live</u>	nosotros <u>vivimos</u>
	you all <u>live</u>	*vosotros <u>vivís</u>*
	they, you all <u>live</u>	ellos, ustedes <u>viven</u>

In the box above, the name of the verb is listed at the top (*to live* / **vivir**) and is called the **infinitive** or the **infinitive form**. This form of the verb is listed in a Spanish language dictionary. **Conjugations** are the different forms of the **infinitive** and reflect who is talking. Both terms, **conjugation** and **infinitive**, will be used throughout **12 Tools for Learning Spanish**.

Personal Pronouns

In English, verbs are always used with personal pronouns (*he walks, she walks, we walk*, etc...). In Spanish, personal pronouns can often be omitted. For example, **yo** is the personal pronoun and **hablo** is the verb. **Yo hablo** and **hablo** both mean *I speak*.

The personal pronouns in English and Spanish are listed below. Some pronouns in Spanish change for gender. **Usted** (*you, formal*) has no equivalent in English and is used to show respect towards the person with whom you are speaking.

Yo	*I*
tú	*you* (informal)
él	*he*
ella	*she*
usted	*you* (formal)
nosotros	*we* (masculine or mixed)
nosotras	*we* (feminine)
ellos	*they* (masculine or mixed)
ellas	*they* (feminine)
ustedes	*you all*
*vosotros	**you all** (used in Spain)

*Vosotros is used exclusively in Spain. Although the verb form for **vosotros** will be listed with the other forms, it will not be featured in the exercises or examples.

Introduction

Using Courtesies: Saying Hello & Goodbye

Courtesies are essential in the Spanish-speaking world. Even if your language abilities are minimal, initiating a conversation or question with *hello* or *good morning* and finishing with *thank you* is very important. Courtesies are part of communicating properly in Spanish.

COURTESY

gracias – *thank you*

de nada – *you're welcome*

no hay de qué – *you're welcome*

con permiso – *with permission, excuse me*

perdón – *excuse me*

mucho gusto – *pleased to meet you*

igualmente – *likewise*

encantado – *charmed*

GREETINGS

buenos días – *good morning*

buenas tardes – *good afternoon*

buenas noches – *good evening*

¿Qué tal? – *what's up?, how's it going?*

¿Cómo estás? (familiar) – *how are you?*

¿Cómo está usted? (formal) – *how are you?*

¿Qué pasa? – *what's happening?*

¿Qué dices? – *what do you say?*

SAYING GOODBYE

adiós – *goodbye*

hasta luego – *see you later (until later)*

hasta pronto – *see you soon*

hasta mañana – *see you tomorrow*

hasta la vista – *until I see you*

hasta la próxima vez – *until next time*

vaya con diós – *go with God*

SECTION 1

POWER TOOLS
CHAPTERS 1-4

Power Tools

SAYING...	TITLE	TOOL	PAGE
1. *I need, I want, I can, can I?*	The Fast Verbs	**Fast Verb + infinitive**	7
2. *I'm going to ...*	The Future	**Ir + a + infinitive**	17
3. *I like it, & I don't like it*	Likes and Dislikes	**Gustar**	23
4. *I have to ...*	Expressing Obligation	**Tener + que + infinitive**	30

Power Tools

NEEDS & WANTS: FAST VERBS

encontrar un banco   *to find* a bank.

comprar dos boletos   *to buy* 2 tickets.

Necesito... *I need*

llamarle a Xuxa   *to call* Xuxa.

🔑 The first **Power Tool** is **Fast Verbs**. They help you get what you want. **Fast Verbs** communicate much, with few words, and are easy to use. There are several **Fast Verbs** (all the **Fast Verbs** are listed at the end of this section). They help you say *I need, I want, I prefer, I can,* and ask questions. **Fast Verbs** have an easy to use formula: **Fast Verb + infinitive**. In any sentence, the **Fast Verb** comes first (1), followed by an **infinitive** (2).[1]

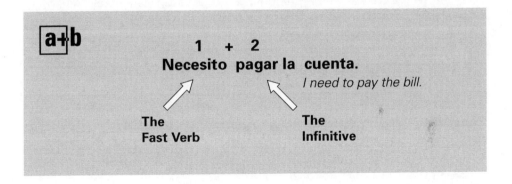

a+b

1 + 2
Necesito pagar la cuenta.

I need to pay the bill.

The
Fast Verb

The
Infinitive

---

1   Remember, an **infinitive**, is a verb before it is changed (conjugated). The **infinitive form** ends in -**ar**, -**er**, or -**ir** (such as **hablar**, **comer**, or **escribir**). See the introduction for a detailed explanation of verbs and words that refer to verbs.

In the sentences below, the **Fast Verb** (**necesitar**) is changed (conjugated) to the **yo** form (**necesito**), and followed by an infinitive (**encontrar**, **comer**, and **hablar**). The meaning of the sentences below changes by simply swapping the infinitive for another infinitive. No conjugation is needed! See the examples with **Necesito**... (*I need*[2]...).

<u>Necesito</u> **encontrar** un banco.	*I need **to find*** a bank.
<u>Necesito</u> **comer** ahora.	*I need **to eat*** now.
<u>Necesito</u> **hablar** español.	*I need **to speak*** Spanish.

Below are examples with another **Fast Verb**, **preferir** (*to prefer*). **Preferir** is especially helpful when we are faced with options. The sentences below follow the pattern of **Fast Verb + infinitive**.

<u>Prefiero</u> **comer** pollo.	*I prefer **to eat*** chicken.
<u>Prefiero</u> **caminar.**	*I prefer **to walk.***
<u>Prefiero</u> **tomar** un taxi.	*I prefer **to take*** a taxi.

Some of the **Fast Verbs** (**necesitar, querer, preferir**) can also be followed by a noun (a person, place, or thing).

<u>Necesito</u> las llaves.	*I need the keys.*
<u>Quiero</u> las fresas.	*I want the strawberries.*
<u>Prefiero</u> los vuelos tempranos.	*I prefer the early flights.*

Poder, deber, and **necesitar** are easy to use for asking questions.

¿<u>Puedo</u> caminar a las pirámides?	***Can I** walk to the pyramids?*
¿<u>Debo</u> hablar con las autoridades?	***Should I** talk with the authorities?*
¿<u>Necesito</u> las llaves?	***Do I** need the keys?*

---

2   The **Fast Verbs** are known as **modals** in English. Most **modals** are used as auxiliary (or helping) verbs. Some **modals** can be used as full verbs when answering short questions (for example, *yes, I do,* or *no, I can't*). For another treatment of **modals** in Spanish, see Warren Hardy's *Power Verbs* (warrenhardy.com).

Power Tools

Some infinitives commonly used with the **Fast Verbs** are listed below.[3]

	en el mercado	**at the market**
Quiero	**comprar**	*to buy*
(*I want*)	**encontrar**	*to find*
	hablar	*to speak*
	comer	*to eat*
	beber	*to drink*
	saber	*to know (a fact/info)*

	en el aeropuerto	**at the airport**
Quiero	**tomar**	*to take*
	esperar	*to wait*
	buscar	*to look for*
	salir	*to leave*
	ir	*to go*
	viajar	*to travel*

	en el hotel	**at the hotel**
Quiero	**dormir**	*to sleep*
	alquilar	*to rent*
	despertarme	*to wake up*
	llamar	*to call*
	viajar	*to travel*
	descansar	*to rest*

	en la casa	**at home**
Quiero	**ver**	*to see*
	leer	*to read*
	escribir	*to write*
	hacer	*to do/make*
	cocinar	*to cook*
	invitar	*to invite*

	en la escuela	**at school**
Quiero	**estudiar**	*to study*
	escuchar	*to listen*
	aprender	*to learn*
	conocer a gente	*meet people*
	conversar	*to converse*
	asistir	*to attend*

---

[3]   For more verbs in the **infinitive form**, see Chapter 41, Most Common Verbs.

Power Tools

Fast Verbs and their forms are listed below.

PODER – *to be able to, can*
puedo	*I*
puedes	*you*
puede	*he, she, Ud.*
podemos	*we*
podéis	*you all*
pueden	*they, you all*

QUERER – *to want*
quiero
quieres
quiere
queremos
queréis
quieren

NECESITAR – *to need*
necesito
necesitas
necesita
necesitamos
necesitáis
necesitan

DEBER – *must, should*
debo
debes
debe
debemos
debéis
deben

PREFERIR – *to prefer*
prefiero
prefieres
prefiere
preferimos
preferís
prefieren

QUISIERA – *would like*
quisiera
quisieras
quisiera
quisiéramos
quisierais
quisieran

Power Tools

FAST VERBS

CONVERSATION

Jeff arrives in León. At the airport he needs to claim his luggage and make his way to San Miguel. He speaks with an agent in the terminal. They are using the **usted** (formal) form.

Jeff: Señor, **quiero** recoger mi maleta. ¿Usted **puede** decirme donde reclamo mi equipaje?

Sir, **I want** to claim my suitcase. **Can** you tell me where I claim my luggage?

El agente: Claro señor, entre usted por esta puerta. También, ¿usted va a querer transportación?

Of course sir, enter through this door. Also, are you going to want transportation?

Jeff: Gracias, y sí. ¿Cómo **puedo** ir a San Miguel?

Thanks, and yes. How **can I** get to San Miguel?

El agente: Puede tomar taxi, o autobús. ¿Cuál **prefiere** usted?

You can take a taxi or bus. Which do you **prefer**?

Jeff: Prefiero el autobús. ¿**Puedo** comprar el boleto de usted?

I prefer the bus. **Can I** buy the ticket from you?

El agente: No señor, se compran los boletos en la ventanilla. ¿**Quiere** usted primera o segunda clase?

No sir, tickets are purchased at the window. **Do you want** first or second class?

Jeff: Prefiero primera clase. ¿Cuánto cuesta?

I prefer first class. How much does it cost?

El agente: Es caro. La primera clase cuesta noventa dólares.

It's expensive. The first class costs ninety dollars.

Jeff: ¡Wow! **Debo** comprar un boleto para la segunda clase. No tengo mucho dinero.

Wow! **I should** buy a ticket for the second class. I don't have much money.

PRACTICE LEVEL 1: FAST VERBS

DIRECTIONS: Conjugate (change) the verbs as needed.

PODER – *to be able to, can*

1) <u>Yo</u> _____ usar la toalla roja.	*<u>I can</u> use the red towel.*
2) ¿<u>Yo</u> _____ bailar contigo?	*<u>Can I</u> dance with you?*
3) <u>Ella</u> _____ venir con nosotros.	*<u>She can</u> come with us.*
4) <u>Nosotros</u> _____ tomar taxi.	*<u>We can</u> take a taxi.*
5) ¿<u>Ellos</u> _____ hablar español?	*<u>Can they</u> speak Spanish?*

NECESITAR – *to need*

6) <u>Yo</u> _____ más agua, por favor.	*<u>I need</u> more water, please.*
7) ¿<u>Tú</u> _____ la dirección?	*Do <u>you need</u> the address?*
8) <u>Nosotros</u> _____ dos boletos.	*<u>We need</u> two tickets.*
9) <u>Ella</u> _____ un boleto.	*<u>She needs</u> a ticket.*
10) <u>Los amigos</u> _____ ayuda.	*The <u>friends need</u> help.*

QUERER – *to want*

11) <u>Yo</u> _____ encontrar la estación.	*<u>I want</u> to find the station.*
12) <u>José</u> _____ los chiles verdes.	*<u>Jose wants</u> the green chiles.*
13) <u>Nosotros</u> _____ pescar temprano.	*<u>We want</u> to fish early.*
14) <u>Ellos</u> _____ un buen desayuno.	*<u>They want</u> a good breakfast.*
15) <u>Las alumnas</u> _____ los textos.	*The <u>students want</u> the text books.*

DEBER – *should, must*

16) <u>Yo</u> _____ comer más frutas frescas.	*<u>I should</u> eat more fresh fruit.*
17) <u>Tú no</u> _____ beber más café.	*<u>You should not</u> drink more coffee.*
18) <u>Linda</u> _____ salir temprano.	*<u>Linda should</u> leave early.*
19) <u>Nosotros</u> _____ comprar gasolina.	*<u>We must</u> buy gasoline.*
20) <u>Los chicos</u> _____ lavarse las manos.	*The <u>boys must</u> wash their hands.*

Power Tools

PREFERIR – *to prefer*

21) <u>Yo</u> _____ el pollo.	<u>*I prefer*</u> *the chicken.*
22) <u>Tú y yo</u> _____ un buen hotel.	<u>*You and I prefer*</u> *a good hotel.*
23) <u>Ella</u> _____ el mar.	<u>*She prefers*</u> *the ocean.*
24) <u>Nosotros</u> _____ las ensaladas.	<u>*We prefer*</u> *the salads.*
25) <u>Ustedes</u> _____ un vuelo corto.	<u>*You all prefer*</u> *a short flight.*

QUISIERA – *would like*

26) <u>Yo</u> _____ ver un menú.	<u>*I would like*</u> *to see a menu.*
27) <u>José</u> _____ comer el pollo.	<u>*Jose would like*</u> *to eat the chicken.*
28) ¿ _____ tú tiempo para decidir?	<u>*Would you like*</u> *time to decide?*
29) <u>Ellos</u> _____ salir ya.	<u>*They would like*</u> *to leave already.*
30) <u>Yo</u> _____ lo mismo.	<u>*I would like*</u> *the same.*

PRACTICE LEVEL 2: FAST VERBS

DIRECTIONS: Answer each question twice according to the cues. Use an infinitive after each **Fast Verb** and more information if necessary.

EXAMPLE

¿Estudias español?	*Do you study Spanish?*
<u>**Necesito estudiar más.**</u>	I need to study more.
<u>**Debo comprar un libro.**</u>	I should buy a book.

1) **¿Quieres viajar a México?**	*Do you want to travel to Mexico?*
_____	I want to travel to Cancún.
_____	I can't go to Mexico.

2) **¿Comes desayuno?**	*Do you eat breakfast?*
_____	I should eat something.
_____	I would like to eat mangos today.

3) **¿Puedes comer con nosotros?**	*Can you eat with us?*
_____	I can eat with you (all).
_____	I should eat with you (all) today.

4) ¿Quieres ir a la playa?
_____
_____

Do you want to go to the beach?
I want to walk to the beach.
Can I go by foot?

5) ¿Tocas un instrumento?
_____
_____

Do you play an instrument?
No, I can't play an instrument.
I would like to play piano.

6) ¿Cocinas huevos?
_____
_____

Do you cook eggs?
I can cook "huevos rancheros."
I need to buy more eggs.

7) ¿Prefieres comer o esperar?
_____
_____

Do you prefer to eat or wait?
I would like to eat now.
I would like to wait an hour.

8) ¿Puedes pagar la cuenta?
_____
_____

Can you pay the bill?
No, I can't pay the bill today.
Yes, I would like to pay with cash.

PRACTICE LEVEL 3: FAST VERBS

DIRECTIONS: Read the answers then figure out what the questions should be. Use **Fast Verbs** in your questions.

EXAMPLE
¿Debes salir ahora_____?
Debo salir ahora.

Should you leave now?
I should leave now.

1) ¿_____?
Sí, quisiera comer carne.

Can you eat meat?
Yes, I would like to eat meat.

2) ¿_____?
Yo quisiera estudiar ahora.

Do you need to study?
I would like to study now.

3) ¿_____?
Prefiero estudiar en la casa.

Can you study outside?
I prefer to study in the house.

4) ¿_____?
Sí, puedo estudiar contigo.

Can you study with me?
Yes, I can study with you.

Power Tools

5) ¿_____?
   Prefiero comer en la cocina.

Where do you want to eat?
I prefer to eat in the kitchen.

6) ¿_____?
   Quiero viajar a Costa Rica.

Where would you like to travel?
I want to travel to Costa Rica.

7) ¿_____?
   Quiero estudiar español.

What do you want to study?
I want to study Spanish.

8) ¿_____?
   Quiero comer huevos.

What do you want to eat?
I want to eat eggs.

9) ¿_____?
   Puedo caminar un poco.

Can you walk a little?
I can walk a little.

10) ¿_____?
    Prefiero comprar pesos.

Do you need to buy pesos?
I prefer to buy pesos.

ANSWERS TO PRACTICE: FAST VERBS

Level 1: Conjugate (change) the verbs as needed.

PODER
1. puedo
2. puedo
3. puede
4. podemos
5. pueden

NECESITAR
6. necesito
7. necesitas
8. necesitamos
9. necesita
10. necesitan

QUERER
11. quiero
12. quiere
13. queremos
14. quieren
15. quieren

DEBER
16. debo
17. debes
18. debe
19. debemos
20. deben

PREFERIR
21. prefiero
22. preferimos
23. prefiere
24. preferimos
25. prefieren

QUISIERA
26. quisiera
27. quisiera
28. quisieras
29. quisieran
30. quisiera

Level 2: Answer each question twice according to the cues. Use an infinitive after each **Fast Verb**, and more information if necessary.

1. Quiero viajar a Cancún.
   No puedo ir a México.

2. Debo comer algo.
   Quiero comer los mangos hoy.

3. Puedo comer con ustedes.
   Debo comer con ustedes hoy.

4. Quiero caminar a la playa.
   ¿Puedo ir a pie?

5. No, no puedo tocar un instrumento.
   Yo quisiera tocar el piano.

6. Puedo cocinar huevos rancheros.
   Necesito comprar más huevos.

7. Prefiero comer ahora.
   Prefiero esperar una hora.

8. No, no puedo pagar la cuenta hoy.
   Sí, quisiera pagar con efectivo.

Level 3: Read the answers, then figure out what the questions should be. Use **Fast Verb**s in your questions.

1. ¿Puedes comer carne?

2. ¿Necesitas estudiar?

3. ¿Puedes estudiar afuera?

4. ¿Puedes estudiar conmigo?

5. ¿Dónde quieres comer?

6. ¿Dónde quisieras viajar?

7. ¿Qué quieres estudiar?

8. ¿Qué quieres comer?

9. ¿Puedes caminar un poco?

10. ¿Necesitas comprar pesos?

Power Tools

THE FUTURE: IR + A + INFINITIVE

Voy a viajar
I'm going to travel

IR
voy
vas
va
vamos
vais
van

When you say you are *going to...* do an activity, you are using the **future**[1] (*I am going to travel, I am going to speak Spanish*). The **future** is frequently used, and easy to form: **Ir + a + infinitive**. By itself, the verb **ir** means *to go*.

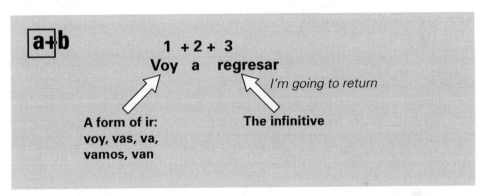

By changing the infinitive (**nadar, cocinar, vivir**), the speaker can change the meaning of the sentence.

Voy a <u>nadar</u>.	*I'm going <u>to swim</u>.*
Voy a <u>cocinar</u>.	*I'm going <u>to cook</u>.*
Voy a <u>vivir</u> aquí.	*I'm going <u>to live</u> here.*

To say someone else is *going to* do something, use a different form of **ir**.

José <u>va</u> a nadar.	*<u>José is</u> going to swim.*
Ellos <u>van</u> a cocinar.	*<u>They are</u> going to cook.*
Tú <u>vas</u> a estudiar.	*<u>You are</u> going to study.*

---

1   The **future** in this chapter is also known as the **informal future**. There is a **future tense** covered in Chapter 13: The Essential Tenses.

Power Tools

USING JUST THE VERB IR

The verb **ir** *(to go)*, can be used separately from the formula **ir + a + infinitive**. **Ir** can be used to say the following:

<u>Voy</u> a la playa.	<u>I go</u> to the beach.
	<u>I am going</u> to the beach.
	<u>I do go</u> to the beach.
<u>Vamos</u> a la escuela.	<u>We go</u> to the school.
	<u>We are going</u> to the school.
	<u>We do go</u> to the school.

When **ir** is used to tell where someone is going, like in the examples above, it is followed by **a** *(to)*. If the word **a** occurs before the article **el** *(the)*, the two words contract to form **al (a + el = al)**. See the examples below.

Ellos van <u>al</u> cine.	They go <u>to the</u> theater.
(a + el = al cine)	They are going <u>to the</u> theater.
	They do go <u>to the</u> theater.
Tú vas <u>al</u> rancho.	You go <u>to the</u> ranch.
(a + el = al rancho)	You are going <u>to the</u> ranch.
	You do go <u>to the</u> ranch.

Power Tools

THE FUTURE: IR + A + INFINITIVE

CONVERSATION

Jeff has met some locals in San Miguel. He is going to make plans to do something this weekend.

Jeff: Hola Julieta. Este sábado **voy a visitar** a un amigo en Los Frailes. ¿Qué **vas a hacer** tú este fin de semana?

Hi Julieta. This Saturday **I am going to visit** a friend in Los Frailes. What **are you going to do** this weekend?

Julieta: **Voy a trabajar** por la mañana.

I am going to work in the morning.

Jeff: Mi amigo tiene un rancho con una piscina. **Vamos a nadar y montar** caballo. ¿No quieres venir después?

My friend has a ranch with a pool. **We are going to swim and ride** horses. You don't want to come by later?

Julieta: Sí me gustaría, pero **no voy a estar** en casa hasta la una.

Yes, I would like to, but I am **not going to be** at home until one o'clock.

Jeff: Está bien. ¿Puedo pasar por tí a la una y media?

That's OK. Can I stop by for you at one thirty?

Julieta: Perfecto, a la una y media. **Voy a estar** lista entonces.

Perfect, at one thirty. **I am going to be** ready then.

Jeff: Excelente. **Vamos a ir** juntos a Los Frailes. Adiós.

Excellent. **We are going to go** together to Los Frailes. Bye.

PRACTICE LEVEL 1: IR (voy, vas, va, vamos, van)

DIRECTIONS: Conjugate **ir** (**voy, vas, va, vamos, van**) as necessary.

1) **Las muchachas _____ a llegar a las seis.**
   The girls are going to arrive at six.

2) **Eduardo y yo _____ a viajar a Lima.**
   Eduardo and I are going to travel to Lima.

3) **Tú _____ a hablar con Juana.**
   You are going to speak with Juana.

4) **Ella _____ a escribir una carta.**
   She is going to write a letter.

5) **Nosotros _____ a comer bien.**
   We are going to eat well.

6) **Los chicos _____ a tomar sodas.**
   The boys are going to drink sodas.

7) **El profesor _____ a enseñar.**
   The teacher is going to teach.

8) **¿Quién _____ a comprar los boletos?**
   Who is going to buy the tickets?

9) **Yo _____ a salir de la fiesta.**
   I am going to leave the party.

10) **Ellas _____ a correr esta mañana.**
    They are going to run this morning.

Power Tools

PRACTICE LEVEL 2: IR + A + INFINITIVE

DIRECTIONS: Answer the questions with the **Future: ir + a + infinitive**.

EXAMPLE

¿Vas a estudiar español?	*Are you going to study Spanish?*
Sí, voy a estudiar español.	*Yes, I'm going to study Spanish.*

1) **¿Vas a nadar?**

_____

Are you going to swim?
Yes, I'm going to swim.

2) **¿Qué vas a hacer hoy?**

_____

What are you going to do today?
I'm going to buy food.

3) **¿Adónde va a estudiar Juan?**

_____

Where is Juan going to study?
Juan is going to study at home.

4) **¿Cuándo van a comer ellos?**

_____

When are they going to eat?
They are going to eat soon.

5) **¿Vas a ir a la playa?**

_____

Are you going to go to the beach?
Yes, I'm going to go to the beach.

6) **¿Vas a visitar la selva?**

_____

Are you going to visit the jungle?
Yes, I'm going to visit the jungle.

7) **¿Cuándo vamos a jugar?**

_____

When are we going to play?
We are going to play today.

8) **¿Quiénes van a venir?**

_____

Who is going to come?
Mario and Ed are going to come.

9) **¿Quién va a llamar?**

_____

Who is going to call?
Omar is going to call.

10) **¿Cuándo vas a dormir?**

_____

When are you going to sleep?
I'm going to sleep soon.

ANSWERS TO PRACTICE: THE FUTURE: IR + A + INFINITIVE

Level 1: Conjugate **ir** (**voy**, **vas**, **va**, **vamos**, **van**) as necessary.

1. van
2. vamos
3. vas
4. va
5. vamos
6. van
7. va
8. va
9. voy
10. van

Level 2: Answer the questions with the **Future: ir + a + infinitive.**

1. Sí, voy a nadar.
2. Voy a comprar comida.
3. Juan va a estudiar en casa.
4. Ellos van a comer pronto.
5. Sí, voy a ir a la playa.
6. Sí, voy a visitar la selva.
7. Vamos a jugar hoy.
8. Mario y Ed van a venir.
9. Omar va a llamar.
10. Voy a dormir pronto.

Power Tools

LIKES & DISLIKES: GUSTAR

Me gusta el taco.
I like the taco.

Gusta is for ONE

Me gustan los tacos.
I like the tacos.

Gustan is for TWO or more

 We use **gustar** to say we like or we don't like something: **Me gusta el hotel** (*I like the hotel*) or, **No me gusta el hotel** (*I don't like the hotel*). Although we use **gustar** to say we like something, the verb actually means *to please*, as in *The popcorn pleases me.* **Gustar** is commonly used with only two verb endings (**gusta**, and **gustan**), and should always be used with a **pronoun (me, te, le, nos, *os*, les).**

Use **gusta** when you like one thing (**Me gusta la playa**, *I like the beach*). Or, use **gusta** with an infinitive when you want to say you like an activity (**Me gusta correr**, *I like to run*). Use **gustan** when you want to say you like more than one thing (**Me gustan las playas**, *I like the beaches*).

The **pronoun** tells who is "liking" something.

Me gusta el libro.
I like the book.

Te gustan los idiomas.
You like the languages.

Le gusta el carro a él.
He likes the car.

Nos gustan los mangos.
We like the mangos.

Les gusta caminar a ellos.
They like to walk.

Les gustan los carros a ustedes.
You all like the cars.

PRONOUNS	
me	*I*
te	*you*
le	*he, she, you formal, it*
nos	*we*
os	*you all*
les	*you all, they*

23

CLARIFICATIONS

Notice that **le** can be used for *he, she,* and *you formal.* As well, **les** can either refer to *they,* or *you all.* If you need to clarify who is being pleased, add **a** and name a person or pronoun at the end or start of the sentence. See the examples below.

Le gusta correr a Juan.	*Juan likes to run.*
A usted le gusta el pastel.	*You (formal) like the cake.*
A ellos les gustan mangos.	*They like the mangos.*
Les gusta bucear a Juan y a David.	*Juan and David like to dive.*

You can also use **gustaría** to soften requests. **Me gustaría** translates to *I would like.* Take a look at the examples below.

Me gustaría comer pescado.	*I would like to eat fish.*
Me gustaría el refresco.	*I would like the soda.*

GUSTAR-LIKE VERBS

There are several other verbs that function in the same way as **gustar**: they only use two forms (singular and plural), and always use a pronoun. These verbs include the following:

parecer	**Me parece bonito.**	*It seems pretty to me.*
to seem	**Me parecen bonitos.**	*They seem pretty to me.*
aburrir	**Te aburre la película.**	*The movie bores you.*
to bore	**Te aburren las películas.**	*The movies bore you.*
encantar	**Le encanta el mango.**	*She loves the mango.*
to "love"	**Le encantan los mangos.**	*She loves the mangos.*
interesar	**Nos interesa el libro.**	*We are interested in the book.*
to interest	**Nos interesan los libros.**	*We are interested in the books.*
faltar	**Les falta una soda.**	*They lack a soda.*
to lack or miss	**Les faltan unas sodas.**	*They lack some sodas.*
fascinar	**Me fascina la salsa.**	*The salsa fascinates me.*
to fascinate	**Me fascinan las salsas.**	*The salsas fascinate me.*

Power Tools

LIKES AND DISLIKES: GUSTAR

CONVERSATION

Jeff and Julieta talk about food.

Julieta: Oye. ¿**Te gustan** los tacos?

Hey. Do **you like** tacos?

Jeff: Sí, **me gustan** los tacos de pescado. Son mis favoritos.

Yes, **I like** the fish tacos. They are my favorites.

Julieta: **Me gustan** los tacos de tripa. ¿**Te gustan** los tacos de tripa? Huelen muy fuerte.

I like the tripe tacos. Do **you like** tripe tacos? They have a strong smell.

Jeff: **No me gusta** la tripa. Comí un taco de cabeza con Javier. **Me gustan** los tacos de pollo. Son ricos.

I don't like tripe. I ate a brain taco with Javier. **I like** the chicken tacos. They're tasty.

Julieta: ¿Qué tal las frutas? ¿Has comido las frutas? A todo el mundo **le gustan** los mangos.

How about fruit? Have you eaten the fruits? **Everyone likes** mangos.

Jeff: Sí, tienes razón, los mangos son ricos. Especialmente **me gusta** el mango manila. A mi amigo **Juan le gustan mucho** los mangos.

Yes, you are right, the mangos are tasty. Especially, **I like** the manila mango. My friend **Juan really likes** mangos.

Julieta: Como **nos gusta** tanto la comida, y es la hora de comer, ¿**Te gustaría** pasar por la taquería?

Since **we like** the food so much, and it is lunch time, **would you like to** stop by the taco shop?

Jeff: Sí, como no. **Me gustaría** ir a la taquería contigo.

Yes, why not. **I would like to** go to the taco shop with you.

PRACTICE LEVEL 1: GUSTA OR GUSTAN

DIRECTIONS: Insert **gusta** or **gustan** in the blanks below.

1) Me _____ las papas.   *I like the potatos.*

2) A ella le _____ el taco.   *She likes the taco.*

3) Nos _____ estudiar español.   *We like to study Spanish.*

4) A Juan le _____ tomar una cerveza.   *Juan likes to drink a beer.*

5) A ustedes les _____ los mariscos.   *You all like seafood.*

6) A los niños les _____ el helado.   *The kids like the ice cream.*

7) Nos _____ la pesca.   *We like fishing.*

8) Me _____ las verduras.   *I like the vegetables.*

9) A ellas les _____ pasar tiempo juntas.   *They like to spend time together.*

10) A mis amigos los _____ tacos de pollo.   *My friends like chicken tacos.*

Power Tools

ME, TE, LE, NOS, OR LES

DIRECTIONS: Fill in the blanks with **me**, **te**, **le**, **nos**, or **les**.

11) **A mí, _____ gusta nadar.**   *I like to swim.*

12) **_____ gustan los deportes a Susana.**   *Susana likes sports.*

13) **_____ gusta viajar en México a nosotros.**   *We like to travel in Mexico.*

14) **¿A tí _____ gusta la birria?**   *Do you like birria?*

15) **A las chicas _____ gustan los clubes.**   *The girls like the clubs.*

16) **A Juana _____ gusta bailar.**   *Juana likes to dance.*

17) **A ustedes _____ gustan los guisantes.**   *You all like the peas.*

18) **_____ gusta el video a mí.**   *I like the video.*

19) **¿A quién _____ gusta el pescado?**   *Who likes fish?*

20) **¿Juanito, _____ gustan los mangos?**   *Juanito, do you like mangos?*

Power Tools

PRACTICE LEVEL 2: GUSTAR

DIRECTIONS: Answer the questions using **gustar** in your answers.

EXAMPLE

¿Te gustan los tacos de pollo?   *Do you like chicken tacos?*
Sí, me gustan los tacos de pollo.   *Yes, I like the chicken tacos.*

1) **¿Te gusta viajar?**   *Do you like to travel?*
   _____   *Yes, I like to travel.*

2) **¿Le gusta el melón a Jorge?**   *Does Jorge like melon?*
   _____   *Yes, Jorge likes the melon.*

3) **¿Les gustan los refrescos a ellos?** *Do they like soft drinks?*
   _____   *Yes, they like soft drinks.*

4) **¿Te gusta el periódico?**   *Do you like the newspaper?*
   _____   *No, I don't like the newspaper.*

5) **¿Le gusta el helado a Susana?**   *Does Susana like ice cream?*
   _____   *No, she doesn't like ice cream.*

6) **¿Te gusta practicar español?**   *Do you like to practice Spanish?*
   _____   *Yes, I like to practice Spanish.*

7) **¿Le gusta la música a ella?**   *Does she like the music?*
   _____   *Yes, she likes the music.*

8) **¿Te gustan los mariscos?**   *Do you like seafood?*
   _____   *Yes, I like seafood.*

9) **¿Te gusta la leche?**   *Do you like milk?*
   _____   *No, I don't like milk.*

10) **¿Le gustan las flores a él?**   *Does he like the flowers?*
    _____   *Yes, he likes the flowers.*

Power Tools

 ANSWERS TO PRACTICE: LIKES AND DISLIKES: GUSTAR

Level 1: Insert **gusta** or **gustan** in the blanks below.

1. gustan
2. gusta
3. gusta
4. gusta
5. gustan
6. gusta
7. gusta
8. gustan
9. gusta
10. gustan

Level 1: Fill in the blanks with **me**, **te**, **le**, **nos**, or **les**.

11. me
12. le
13. nos
14. te
15. les
16. le
17. les
18. me
19. le
20. te

Level 2: Answer the questions using **gustar** in your answers.

1. Sí, me gusta viajar.

2. Sí, le gusta el melón a Jorge.

3. Sí, a ellos les gustan los refrescos.

4. No, no me gusta el periódico.

5. No, a ella no le gusta el helado.

6. Sí, me gusta practicar el español.

7. Sí, a ella le gusta la música.

8. Sí, me gustan los mariscos.

9. No, no me gusta la leche.

10. Sí, le gustan las flores a él.

EXPRESSING OBLIGATION: TENER+QUE+INFINITIVE

estudiar mucho.
study a lot.

comer bien.
eat well.

dormir ocho horas.
sleep eight hours.

Tengo que...
I have to...

TENER
tengo
tienes
tiene
tenemos
tienéis
tienen

To say I *have to* (I *have to* eat, I *have to* leave), use the formula, **tener + que + infinitive**. This is another easy 1, 2, 3 construction. By itself, the verb **tener** means *to have*.

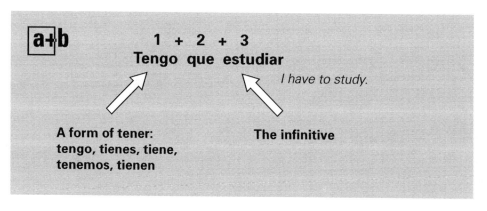

a+b

1 + 2 + 3
Tengo que estudiar

I have to study.

A form of tener:
tengo, tienes, tiene,
tenemos, tienen

The infinitive

To change the meaning of the sentence, the speaker changes the infinitive (**investigar, enseñar, leer**).

Tengo que <u>investigar</u>.	*I have <u>to investigate</u>.*
Tengo que <u>enseñar</u>.	*I have <u>to teach</u>.*
Tengo que <u>leer</u>.	*I have <u>to read</u>.*

To say someone else has to do something, use a different form of **tener**.

<u>Tú tienes</u> que salir.	*<u>You have</u> to leave.*
<u>Ella tiene</u> que trabajar.	*<u>She has</u> to work.*
<u>Ellos tienen</u> que descansar.	*<u>They have</u> to rest.*

Power Tools

USING JUST THE VERB TENER

The verb **tener** *(to have)*, can be used separately from the formula **tener** + **que** + **infinitive**. **Tener** can be used to say the following:

Tengo un carro.	*I have a car.*
Ella tiene la hora.	*She has the time.*
Tenemos muchos pesos.	*We have a lot of pesos.*
Ellos tienen un taxi.	*They have a taxi.*

There are several common idioms that use the verb **tener**. To use these expressions, the speaker usually conjugates **tener**.

tener ___ años	*to be ___ years old*
tener miedo	*to be scared*
tener sed	*to be thirsty*
tener hambre	*to be hungry*
tener ganas de	*to feel like*
tener sueño	*to be sleepy*
tener razón	*to be right*
tener frío	*to be cold*
tener calor	*to be hot*
tener prisa	*to be in a hurry*
tener cuidado	*to be careful*

Power Tools

EXPRESSING OBLIGATION

CONVERSATION

Jeff has things to do. Juan and Jeff talk about what has to be done for school.

Juan: **Tienes que estar** bien preparado para el primer día de clases.

You have to be well prepared for the first day of classes.

Jeff: ¿Qué **tengo que hacer**?

What do **I have to do**?

Juan: Primero, **tienes que averiguar** cuál autobús va a la universidad. También, **tienes que llevar** tu mochila y horario de clases.

First, **you have to figure out** which bus goes to the university. Also, **you have to carry** your backpack and class schedule.

Jeff: ¿**Tienes que sacar** un carnet antes de empezar clases?

Do **you have to get** an ID card before starting classes?

Juan: Sí, podemos sacar carnets juntos. Debemos llegar temprano. **Tenemos que pagar** con efectivo.

Yes, we can get ID's together. We should arrive early. **We have to pay** with cash.

Jeff: Con tanto que hacer, **tengo que despertarme** temprano.

With so much to do, **I have to get up** early.

Juan: Sí, vamos a estar muy ocupados los próximos meses.

Yes, we are going to be very busy for the next few months.

Power Tools

PRACTICE LEVEL 1: TENER

DIRECTIONS: Fill in the blanks with a form of **tener**.

1) **Los chicos _____ que comer las verduras.**
   The boys have to eat the vegetables.

2) **Mi amigo _____ que comprar una camisa.**
   My friend has to buy a shirt.

3) **Ella _____ que regresar pronto.**
   She has to return soon.

4) **Tú _____ que leer español conmigo.**
   You have to read Spanish with me.

5) **Nosotros _____ que salir a las seis en punto.**
   We have to leave at six sharp.

6) **Oscar y Manolo _____ que hacer las tortillas.**
   Oscar and Manolo have to make the tortillas.

7) **Benigno _____ que pintar las puertas.**
   Benigno has to paint the doors.

8) **La profesora _____ que dar una clase por la mañana.**
   The teacher has to give a class in the morning.

9) **Yo _____ que ver a mi mamá.**
   I have to see my mother.

10) **Los amigos _____ que viajar con sus padres.**
    The friends have to travel with their parents.

PRACTICE LEVEL 2: TENER + QUE + INFINITIVE

DIRECTIONS: Answer the questions with **tener + que + infinitive**.

EXAMPLE

    ¿Tienes que estudiar español?   *Do you have to study Spanish?*

    <u>**Sí, tengo que estudiar español.**</u>   *Yes, I have to study Spanish.*

1) **¿Tienen que comer ya?**   *Do they have to eat already?*
    _____   *Yes, they have to eat.*

2) **¿Qué tiene que hacer Juan?**   *What does Juan have to do?*
    _____   *Juan has to go to the airport.*

3) **¿Adónde tienes que ir?**   *Where do you have to go?*
    _____   *I have to go home.*

4) **¿Cuándo tienes que regresar?**   *When do you have to return?*
    _____   *I have to return tomorrow.*

5) **¿Tenemos que salir ya?**   *Do we have to leave already?*
    _____   *No, we don't have to leave.*

6) **¿Quién tiene que hacer tarea?**   *Who has to do homework?*
    _____   *I have to do homework.*

7) **¿Tienes que pagar con efectivo?**   *Do you have to pay with cash?*
    _____   *No, I have to pay with a credit card.*

8) **¿Tienes que escribir un email?**   *Do you have to write an email?*
    _____   *Yes, I have to write an email.*

9) **¿Quién tiene que cocinar?**   *Who has to cook?*
    _____   *Lalo has to cook.*

10) **¿Tienes que comprar comida?**   *Do you have to buy food?*
    _____   *Yes, I have to buy food.*

Power Tools

 ANSWERS TO PRACTICE: EXPRESSING OBLIGATION

Level 1: Fill in the blanks with a form of **tener**.

1. tienen
2. tiene
3. tiene
4. tienes
5. tenemos
6. tienen
7. tiene
8. tiene
9. tengo
10. tienen

Level 2: Answer the questions with **tener + que + infinitive**.

1. Sí, tienen que comer.
2. Juan tiene que ir al aeropuerto.
3. Tengo que ir a la casa.
4. Tengo que regresar mañana.
5. No, no tenemos que salir.
6. Tengo que hacer la tarea.
7. No, tengo que pagar con una tarjeta de crédito.
8. Sí, tengo que escribir un email.
9. Lalo tiene que cocinar.
10. Sí, tengo que comprar comida.

SECTION 2

HAND TOOLS
CHAPTERS 5-8

Hand Tools

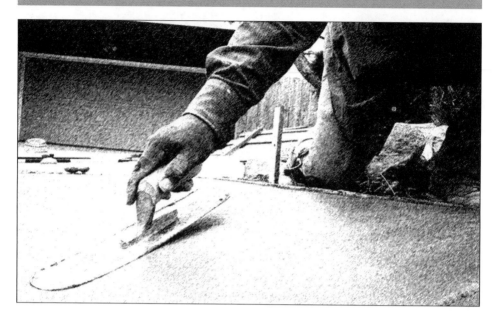

SAYING...	TITLE	TOOL	PAGE
5. *I am from ___, I am a ___, I am the ___...*	Identifying origin, characteristics, occupation, and relationships	**Ser**	38
6. *I am in ___, I feel ___*	Describing Condition & Telling Location	**Estar**	43
7. *I, you, him, her, us, they, etc.*	Object Pronouns: People & Things	**Lo, la, los, las, me, te, le, nos, les, etc.**	49
8. *Telling & asking what is around you*	There Is / There Are	**Hay**	60

IDENTIFYING ORIGIN, CHARACTERISTICS, OCCUPATION, & RELATIONSHIPS: SER

SER
soy
eres
es
somos
sois
son

Soy de Baja.   origin
  I am from Baja.

Soy muy positivo.   characteristics
  I am very positive.

Soy maestro.   occupation
  I am a teacher.

Soy el papá de dos niños.   relationship
  I am the father of two children.

Ser is one of two verbs in Spanish that mean, *to be* (the other is **estar**).

🔧 **Ser** is used to identify and describe **origin**, **characteristics**, **occupation**, and **relationships**.

(1) ORIGIN

Soy de California.
  I am from California.
Tú eres de Cuba.
  You are from Cuba.
¿Ustedes son de aquí?
  Are you all from here?

(2) CHARACTERISTICS

Soy un hombre alto.
  I am a tall man.
Eres muy divertida.
  You are very fun.
Ellos son muy serios.
  They are very serious.

(3) OCCUPATION

Lorenzo es el profesor.
  Lorenzo is the teacher.
Mita es la abogada.
  Mita is the lawyer.
Lorena es dentista.
  Lorena is a dentist.

(4) RELATIONSHIPS

Flora es una amiga mía.
  Flora is a friend of mine.
Juan es mi tío.
  Juan is my uncle.
Texas es un estado en mi país.
  Texas is a state in my country.

SER

CONVERSATION

Jeff and Julieta are telling about themselves and their families.

Jeff: Yo **soy** de Montana. **Soy** de una familia grande. Tengo tres hermanas y tres hermanos. Mis hermanos **son** altos. Mis hermanas **son** bajas.

I **am** from Montana. **I am** from a large family. I have three sisters and three brothers. My brothers **are** tall. My sisters **are** short.

Julieta: No tengo hermanos. Mi papá **es** bajo y mi mamá **es** alta. Ellos **son** de Acapulco. Yo **soy** como mi papá, bajita.

I don't have brothers and sisters. My dad **is** short and my mom **is** tall. They **are** from Acapulco. **I am** like my dad, short.

Jeff: Mi papá **es** artista. Escribe mucho y pinta. El **es** muy artístico. **Es** un hombre simpático y divertido.

My dad **is** an artist. He writes a lot and paints. He **is** very artistic. He **is** a nice and fun guy.

Julieta: Mi mamá **es** dentista. Mi mamá y papá hacen una pareja muy buena. Ellos **son** muy felices.

My mom **is** a dentist. My mom and dad make a very good couple. They **are** very happy.

Jeff: ¿**Es** Romero tu primo?

Is Romero your cousin?

Julieta: Sí, él **es** el hijo de mi tío Arnulfo.

Yes, he **is** the son of my uncle Arnulfo.

Hand Tools

 PRACTICE LEVEL 1: SER

DIRECTIONS: Fill in the blanks with a form of **ser**.

1) Yo _____ Juan Uribe.   *I am Juan Uribe.*

2) Tú _____ un buen muchacho.   *You are a good boy.*

3) Ellas _____ de México.   *They are from Mexico.*

4) La familia _____ amable.   *The family is nice.*

5) ¿Ustedes _____ de aquí?   *You all are from here?*

6) Yo _____ un estudiante.   *I am a student.*

7) Nosotros _____ americanos.   *We are American.*

8) Xuxa _____ mi esposa.   *Xuxa is my wife.*

9) ¿_____ ella dentista?   *Is she a dentist?*

10) Las chicas _____ listas.   *The girls are smart.*

11) Tú _____ una muchacha alta.   *You are a tall girl.*

12) Susana _____ una amiga de Ben.   *Susana is a friend of Ben.*

13) Nosotros _____ altos y guapos.   *We are tall and handsome.*

14) Ella _____ la cocinera.   *She is the cook.*

15) Lorenzo _____ el primo de Lalo.   *Lorenzo is the cousin of Lalo.*

PRACTICE LEVEL 2: SER

DIRECTIONS: Use a form of **ser** in each answer.

1) **¿De dónde eres?**
   Yo _____ de California.

   Where are you from?
   I am from California.

2) **¿Quién es ella?**
   Ella _____ una amiga de Juan.

   Who is she?
   She is a friend of Juan.

3) **¿Cómo es Julia?**
   Ella _____ honesta, divertida, y amable.

   What is Julia like?
   She is honest, fun, and nice.

4) **¿Quiénes son ellas?**
   Ellas _____ mis amigas.

   Who are they (fem.)?
   They are my friends.

5) **¿Eres muy alto?**
   Sí, _____ muy alto.

   Are you very tall?
   Yes, I am very tall.

6) **¿Cómo es Jorge?**
   Jorge _____ bajo y fuerte.

   What is Jorge like?
   Jorge is short and strong.

7) **¿De dónde son ustedes?**
   Nosotros _____ de los Estados Unidos.

   Where are you all from?
   We are from the United States.

8) **¿Quiénes son ellos?**
   Ellos _____ doctores y enfermeras.

   Who are they?
   They are doctors and nurses.

9) **¿Quién eres?**
   Yo _____ Pat Smith.

   Who are you?
   I am Pat Smith.

10) **¿Cuál hombre es Chato?**
    Chato _____ el hombre amable.

    Which man is Chato?
    Chato is the nice guy.

ANSWERS TO PRACTICE: SER

Level 1: Fill in the blanks with a form of **ser**.

1. soy
2. eres
3. son
4. es
5. son
6. soy
7. somos
8. es
9. es
10. son
11. eres
12. es
13. somos
14. es
15. es

Level 2: Use a form of **ser** in each answer.

1. soy
2. es
3. es
4. son
5. soy
6. es
7. somos
8. son
9. soy
10. es

Hand Tools

DESCRIBING CONDITION & TELLING LOCATION: ESTAR

Estoy contento hoy. condition
I am happy today.

Estoy en la casa. location
I am at home.

ESTAR
estoy
estás
está
estamos
estáis
están

Estar is the second of two verbs that mean, *to be* (the other is **ser**).

Estar is used to describe the **condition of people and things** (well, sick, nervous, new, used, tattered, polished, etc.), and to **tell where people and things are located**.

(1) DESCRIBING CONDITION

Estoy bien, gracias.
I am fine, thanks.
Estás muy animado.
You are very excited.
El carro está usado.
The car is used.
¿Estamos listos?
Are we ready?

(2) TELLING LOCATION

Las montañas están en Perú.
The mountains are in Peru.
Luisa está en el garaje.
Luisa is in the garage.
Maira y Luis están aquí.
Maira and Luis are here.
¿Dónde está el hotel?
Where is the hotel?

Hand Tools

DESCRIBING CONDITION & TELLING LOCATION: ESTAR

CONVERSATION

Jeff is not feeling so well. He speaks to Dr. Vargas by phone.

Jeff: Dr. Vargas, **estoy** enfermo.

Dr. Vargas, **I am** sick.

Dr. Vargas: ¿Cuáles son tus síntomas?

What are your symptoms?

Jeff: Tengo dolor de cabeza. **Estoy** cansado. También me duele el estómago. Fui a Tacos Manuel anoche. Pasé la noche en la casa de un amigo.

I have a headache. **I am** tired. Also, my stomach hurts. I went to Tacos Manuel last night. I spent the night at the house of a friend.

Dr. Vargas: ¿Dónde **estás** ahora?

Where **are you** now?

Jeff: **Estoy** en mi departamento.

I am in my apartment.

Dr. Vargas: Sí Jeff, **estás** enfermo. ¿Puedes venir al consultorio? ¿Sabes dónde **está** mi oficina?

Yes Jeff, you **are** sick. Can you come to the office? Do you know where my office **is**?

Jeff: **Está** en el centro, ¿verdad?

It is downtown, right?

Dr. Vargas: Sí, **está** en frente del centro comercial.

Yes, **it's** across from the mall.

Hand Tools

 PRACTICE LEVEL 1: ESTAR

DIRECTIONS: Insert a conjugation of **estar** in each blank below.

1) ¿Dónde _____ la casa?   *Where is the house?*

2) Yo _____ en Nicaragua.   *I am in Nicaragua.*

3) El mercado _____ en la Calle Sexta.   *The market is on Sixth Street.*

4) La Gloria _____ en las montañas.   *La Gloria is in the mountains.*

5) ¿Dónde _____ las muchachas?   *Where are the girls?*

6) ¿Cómo _____ tú?   *How are you?*

7) La cena _____ caliente.   *The dinner is hot.*

8) ¿ _____ tú en el parque?   *Are you in the park?*

9) Adrian _____ enfermo.   *Adrian is sick.*

10) ¿Cuándo _____ tú en la oficina?   *When are you in the office?*

11) Los hermanos no _____ aquí.   *The brothers are not here.*

12) Yo _____ cansado hoy.   *I am tired today.*

13) El perro _____ en la casa.   *The dog is in the house.*

14) Nadie _____ allí.   *Nobody is there.*

15) La sopa _____ fría ya.   *The soup is cold already.*

Hand Tools

PRACTICE LEVEL 2: ESTAR

DIRECTIONS: Insert a form of **estar** in the spaces below.

1) **¿Dónde está el hotel Ritz?**
   El hotel _____ en el sur.

   Where is the Ritz hotel?
   The hotel is in the south.

2) **¿Dónde estás ahora?**
   _____ en la casa de Jaime.

   Where are you now?
   I am at Jaime's house.

3) **¿Cómos estás?**
   Yo _____ bien, gracias.

   How are you?
   I am fine, thanks.

4) **¿Cómo están las chicas?**
   Ellas _____ felices y cansadas.

   How are the girls?
   They are happy and tired.

5) **¿Dónde están las montañas?**
   Las montañas _____ en México.

   Where are the mountains?
   The mountains are in Mexico.

6) **¿Quién está en la escuela?**
   Mi niño _____ en la escuela.

   Who is in the school?
   My child is in the school.

7) **¿Quiénes están en la playa?**
   Todos _____ en la playa.

   Who is at the beach?
   Everyone is at the beach.

8) **¿Dónde están los primos?**
   Ellos _____ en la escuela.

   Where are the cousins?
   They are at school.

9) **¿Cómo está el agua?**
   El agua _____ fría todavía.

   How is the water?
   The water is still cold.

10) **¿Dónde está el estadio?**
    El estadio _____ en la costa.

    Where is the stadium?
    The stadium is on the coast.

PRACTICE LEVEL 3: ESTAR OR SER

DIRECTIONS: Fill the blanks below with a form of either **estar** or **ser**.

1) **Los amigos _____ en California.**
   The friends are in California.

2) **Ellos _____ de Ibiza.**
   They are from Ibiza.

3) **Juana y Carlos _____ tristes porque van a regresar mañana.**
   Juan and Carlos are sad because they are going to return tomorrow.

4) **¿Dónde _____ Juan?**
   Where is Juan?

5) **Tú _____ inteligente y divertida.**
   You are intelligent and fun.

6) **Todos mis amigos _____ en Puerto Vallarta.**
   All of my friends are in Puerto Vallarta.

7) **No me siento bien, yo _____ enfermo.**
   I don't feel well, I am sick.

8) **¿Dónde vas a _____ este verano?**
   Where are you going to be this summer?

9) **¿Quién _____ él?**
   Who is he?

10) **Yo _____ alto, fuerte, listo, y humilde.**
    I am tall, strong, smart, and humble.

ANSWERS TO PRACTICE: ESTAR

Level 1: Insert a conjugation of **estar** in each blank below.

1. está
2. estoy
3. está
4. está
5. están
6. estás
7. está
8. estás
9. está
10. estás
11. están
12. estoy
13. está
14. está
15. está

Level 2: Insert a form of **estar** in the spaces below.

1. está
2. estoy
3. estoy
4. están
5. están
6. está
7. están
8. están
9. está
10. está

Level 3: Fill the blanks below with a form of either **estar** or **ser**.

1. están
2. son
3. están
4. está
5. eres
6. están
7. estoy
8. estar
9. es
10. soy

OBJECT PRONOUNS: PEOPLE & THINGS

✎ **Object pronouns** are words used in place of nouns. *Him, her, me, you, it,* and *them* are all **object pronouns**. If we say, *I give the shoe to <u>him</u>,* instead of, *I give the shoe to <u>Bob</u>,* we are substituting a **pronoun** *(him)* for a noun *(Bob).*

There are two groups of **object pronouns: direct object pronouns**, and **indirect object pronouns**. Figuring out which is appropriate, direct or indirect, takes practice. The shortcut[1] to using **object pronouns** is this…

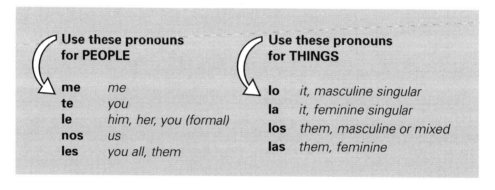

Use these pronouns for PEOPLE		Use these pronouns for THINGS	
me	*me*	**lo**	*it, masculine singular*
te	*you*	**la**	*it, feminine singular*
le	*him, her, you (formal)*	**los**	*them, masculine or mixed*
nos	*us*	**las**	*them, feminine*
les	*you all, them*		

PEOPLE

<u>Me</u> compras un mango.

   You buy <u>me</u> a mango.

<u>Le</u> doy los boletos a ella.[2]

   I give <u>her</u> the tickets.

THINGS

Quieren cocinar<u>los</u> en casa. (los = los tacos)

   They want to cook them at home.

Estoy comprándo<u>la</u> ahora. (la = la casa)

   I am buying it now.

---

1   The shortcut listed above is accurate for most cases. To gain a better understanding and more precision with **object pronouns**, it is necessary to be able to distinguish between **direct** and **indirect objects**. See the following page for more information.

2   **Le** can mean *her* or *him* and in some instances might be ambiguous. At the end of the sentence, **a ella** clarifies to whom the tickets are given. Even though it might seem sufficient to write **Doy los boletos a ella**, it is preferable to use both **le** and the clarifier **a ella** (Le doy los boletos a ella).

Hand Tools

DIRECT & INDIRECT OBJECTS

In the small percentage of cases in which the shortcut does not work, being able to distinguish between **direct** and **indirect objects** is essential for choosing the correct **object pronoun**. See below.

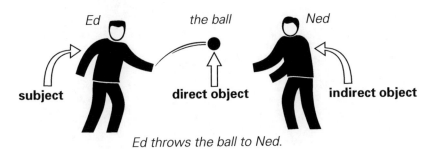

Ed throws the ball to Ned.

In the sentence, *Ed throws the ball to Ned*, *Ed* is the **subject**, *the ball* is the **direct object**, and *Ned* is the **indirect object**.

THE SUBJECT

<u>The agent (usually a person) doing the activity</u> in a sentence. Above, *Ed* is throwing the ball. *Ed* is the **subject**.

THE DIRECT OBJECT

The **direct object** receives the action of the verb. <u>It is the thing that is given, thrown, told, sold, seen, and so on</u>. When someone is getting something from someone else, the **direct object** is what passes from one person to another.

Identifying the **direct object**
1. Find the verb (*throws*).
2. Use the verb to ask *what* or *who* (*throws what?* or *throws who?*).
3. The answer to the question above is the **direct object** (*throws what? the ball*). *The ball* is the **direct object**.

THE INDIRECT OBJECT

The **indirect object** <u>is the agent (usually a person) that is receiving something</u>. Above, *Ned* is receiving the ball. *Ned* is the **indirect object**.

Identifying the **indirect object**
1. The destination of the **direct object** is the **indirect object**.
2. The **indirect object** tells *to whom* or *for whom* the action of the verb is done (*To whom* is the ball thrown? The ball is thrown to *Ned*). *Ned* is the **indirect object**.

51

The complete list of object pronouns appears in the table below.

DIRECT OBJECT PRONOUNS

me	*me*
te	*you*
lo	*it, him, you formal*
la	*it, her, you formal*
nos	*us*
os	*you all*
los	*them, you all*
las	*them, you all*

INDIRECT OBJECT PRONOUNS

me	*me*
te	*you*
le	*him, her, you formal*
nos	*us*
os	*you all*
les	*them, you all*

PLACING PRONOUNS IN SENTENCES

When using object pronouns, it is essential to know where they can be placed in a sentence. There are only three possible positions.

1. BEFORE THE CONJUGATED VERB

Ella <u>te</u> va a llamar.	*She is going to call <u>you</u>.*
<u>Les</u> necesito felicitar.	*I need to congratulate <u>them</u>.*

2. ATTACHED TO AN INFINITIVE

Ella va a llamar<u>te</u>.	*She is going to call <u>you</u>.*
Quiero comprar<u>la</u>.	*I want to buy <u>it</u>.* **(la = la playera)**

3. ATTACHED TO THE "-ING" ENDING[3]

this placement requires an accent on the stressed syllable

Estoy llamándo<u>te</u>.	*I am calling <u>you</u>.*
El está tocándo<u>lo</u>.	*He is playing <u>it</u>.* **(lo = el piano)**

---

[3]   For more about the "-ing" ending, see Chapter 25: Present Progessive.

Hand Tools

DOUBLE OBJECT PRONOUNS

When both **direct object** and **indirect object pronouns** are used in one sentence, they are often referred to as **double object pronouns**. They always occur in the order "**ID**," **I**ndirect then **D**irect, as we read left to right. They are never separated.

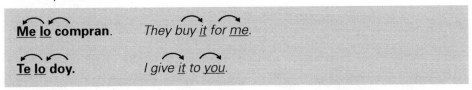

Me lo compran.   *They buy it for me.*

Te lo doy.   *I give it to you.*

✎ Notice that the English and Spanish examples above make mirror images (look at the direction of the arrows): verb and pronoun placement is reversed.

SUBSTITUTING "SE" IN DOUBLE OBJECT PRONOUNS

When a combination of **double object pronouns** begins with **le** or **les** (**le lo**..., or **les las**...), the first pronoun must be changed to **se**.

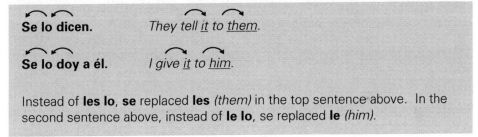

Se lo dicen.   *They tell it to them.*

Se lo doy a él.   *I give it to him.*

Instead of **les lo**, **se** replaced **les** *(them)* in the top sentence above. In the second sentence above, instead of **le lo**, se replaced **le** *(him)*.

Notice, **a él** is used after the sentence to clarify the meaning of **se**, similar to the clarifications used for verbs like **gustar**.

OBJECT PRONOUNS: PEOPLE & THINGS

CONVERSATION

Jeff has to explain.

Jeff: Anoche **le** di mi libro a Juana. Poco después, ella salió para su casa.

Last night I gave my book to Juana. Shortly thereafter she left for her house.

Juan: Creo que **le** diste mi libro a ella. Si te acuerdas, **te lo** presté.

I think you gave **her** my book. If you remember, I loaned **it to you**.

Jeff: ¿**Me lo** prestaste? **Me** regalaste el libro. ¿No?

You loaned **it to me**? You gave **me** the book. No?

Juan: No. Iba a prestar**lo** a Juana. Pero, al final de cuentas, **te lo** presté. Tienes que pedír**selo**. **Lo** voy a necesitar pronto.

No. I was going to loan **it** to Juana. But, at the end of the day, I loaned **it to you**. You have to ask **her for it**. I am going to need **it** soon.

Jeff: ¿Sabes qué? Acabo de hablar con ella y **se lo** dio a su hermano Blas.

You know what? I just spoke with her and she gave **it to her** brother Blas.

Juan: ¡Qué suerte! **Lo** voy a ver esta noche. **Lo** veré en el café. ¿**Lo** traerá?

What luck! I am going to see **him** tonight. I will see **him** in the café. Will he bring **it**?

Jeff: ¿Quién sabe? **Lo** dudo.

Who knows? I doubt **it**.

Hand Tools

 PRACTICE LEVEL 1: OBJECT PRONOUNS

DIRECTIONS: Fill in the blanks with **me**, **te**, **le**, **nos**, or **les**. Use the sentence in English as a guide.

1) **Benito ____ da un regalo.**   *Benito gives me a gift.*

2) **Tú ____ compras un libro.**   *You buy him a book.*

3) **Ellos ____ dan la tarea.**   *They give you the homework.*

4) **Yo ____ regalo los videos.**   *I gift you all the videos.*

5) **Silia ____ cocina pollo.**   *Silia cooks us chicken.*

6) **Yo ____ digo mis secretos a ellos.**   *I tell my secrets to them.*

7) **Las chicas ____ dan los tacos.**   *The girls give me the tacos.*

8) **Nosotros ____ contamos los chistes.**   *We tell you the jokes.*

9) **Ellos ____ compran todo.**   *They buy them everything.*

10) **Jason ____ cuenta los datos a ella.**   *Jason tells her the data.*

11) **Nadie ____ da nada.**   *Nobody gives me anything.*

12) **El novio ____ compra un anillo a ella.**   *The boyfriend buys her a ring.*

13) **Tú ____ debes mucho dinero.**   *You owe me a lot of money.*

14) **Bob ____ da el pescado.**   *Bob gives us the fish.*

15) **Tula ____ va a llamar.**   *Tula is going to call us.*

PRACTICE LEVEL 2: DIRECT OBJECT PRONOUNS (LO, LA, LOS, LAS)

DIRECTIONS: Substitute the **direct object** with a **direct object pronoun (lo, la, los, las)**.

1) Como <u>las tortillas</u> con salsa.
   _____ como con salsa.

I eat <u>the tortillas</u> with salsa.
I eat <u>them</u> with salsa.

2) Voy a comer <u>el mango</u>.
   _____ voy a comer.

I am going to eat <u>the mango</u>.
I am going to eat <u>it</u>.

3) Ella limpia <u>la casa</u>.
   Ella _____ limpia.

She cleans <u>the house</u>.
She cleans <u>it</u>.

4) Ellos estudian <u>los libros</u>.
   Ellos _____ estudian.

They study <u>the books</u>.
They study <u>them</u>.

5) Flavia deposita <u>el dinero</u>.
   Flavia _____ deposita.

Flavia deposits <u>the money</u>.
Flavia deposits <u>it</u>.

6) Tú escribes <u>libros</u> todavía.
   Tú _____ escribes todavía.

You still write <u>books</u>.
You still write <u>them</u>.

7) Gigi planea <u>la fiesta</u>.
   Gigi _____ planea.

Gigi plans <u>the party</u>.
Gigi plans <u>it</u>.

8) Escribo <u>cartas</u> a menudo.
   _____ escribo a menudo.

I write <u>letters</u> often.
I write <u>them</u> often.

9) Me describes <u>las casas</u>.
   Me _____ describes.

You describe <u>the houses</u> to me.
You describe <u>them</u> to me.

10) La tienda tiene <u>la batería</u>.
   La tienda _____ tiene.

The store has <u>the battery</u>.
The store has <u>it</u>.

Hand Tools

PRACTICE LEVEL 2: DIRECT OBJECT PRONOUNS (LO, LA, LOS, LAS)

DIRECTIONS: Replace the underlined **direct objects** in the question with **direct object pronouns** in the answer. Use **DOP's** in your responses (**lo**, **la**, **los**, **las**).

EXAMPLE

   ¿Quieres comer <u>las uvas</u>?   *Do you want to eat <u>the grapes</u>?*
     Sí, <u>las</u> quiero comer.   *Yes, I want to eat <u>them</u>.*

1) ¿Comes <u>la carne</u>?

  _____   *Do you eat <u>meat</u>?*
                                          Yes, I eat <u>it</u>.

2) ¿Bebes mucho <u>té</u>?

  _____   *Do you drink a lot of <u>tea</u>?*
                                          No, I don't drink <u>it</u> much.

3) ¿Ellos comen <u>los tacos</u>?

  _____   *Do they eat <u>the tacos</u>?*
                                          Yes, they eat <u>them</u>.

4) ¿Ella compra <u>las camisas</u>?

  _____   *Does she buy <u>the shirts</u>?*
                                          No, she doesn't buy <u>them</u>.

5) ¿Ellos leen <u>los libros</u>?

  _____   *Do they read <u>the books</u>?*
                                          Yes, they read <u>them</u>.

6) ¿Escribes <u>cartas</u>?

  _____   *Do you write <u>letters</u>?*
                                          No, I don't write <u>them</u>.

7) ¿Tienes <u>la información</u>?

  _____   *Do you have <u>the information</u>?*
                                          Yes, I have <u>it</u>.

8) ¿Ves <u>al señor</u>?

  _____   *Do you see <u>the man</u>?*
                                          Yes, I see <u>him</u>.

9) ¿Quieres comer <u>unas gorditas</u>?

  _____   *Do you want to eat some <u>gorditas</u>?*
                                          Yes, I want to eat <u>them</u>.

10) ¿Quieres cocinar <u>el flan</u>?

  _____   *Do you want to cook <u>the flan</u>?*
                                          Yes, I want to cook <u>it</u>.

PRACTICE LEVEL 3: INDIRECT OBJECT PRONOUNS
(ME, TE, LE, NOS, OR LES)

DIRECTIONS: Read the questions carefully, then answer with **me**, **te**, **le**, **nos**, or **les**.

EXAMPLE

¿Juan <u>te</u> dice el secreto?   *Juan tells <u>you</u> the secret?*
<u>**Sí, Juan me dice el secreto.**</u>   *Yes, Juan tells <u>me</u> the secret.*

1) **¿Raúl <u>nos</u> vende el libro?**

_____   *Raúl sells <u>us</u> the book?*
No, Raúl doesn't sell <u>us</u> the book.

2) **¿<u>Les</u> invitas la cena?**

_____   *Are you buying <u>them</u> dinner?*
Yes, I am buying <u>them</u> dinner.

3) **¿Ellos <u>te</u> dan el dinero?**

_____   *They give <u>you</u> the money?*
Yes, they give <u>me</u> the money.

4) **¿Ustedes <u>les</u> hacen desayuno?**   *Do you (all) make <u>them</u> breakfast?*

_____   *Yes, we make <u>them</u> breakfast.*

5) **¿<u>Te</u> dan la llanta?**   *Are they giving <u>you</u> the tire?*

_____   *Yes, they are giving <u>me</u> the tire.*

6) **¿<u>Nos</u> compras las bebidas?**   *Are you buying <u>us</u> the drinks?*

_____   *Yes, I'm buying <u>you all</u> the drinks.*

7) **¿<u>Nos</u> dicen la información?**   *Do they tell <u>us</u> the information?*

_____   *No, they don't tell <u>us</u> anything.*

Hand Tools

PRACTICE LEVEL 3: DIRECT OBJECTS & INDIRECT OBJECTS WITH DOUBLE OBJECT PRONOUNS

DIRECTIONS: Substitute both the **direct objects** and **indirect objects** with **double object pronouns**.

1) **Juan le da un libro a Julia.**
   _____

   Juan gives the book to Julia.
   Juan gives it to her.

2) **Lalo le dice el secreto a Chato.**
   _____

   Lalo tells the secret to Chato.
   Lalo tells it to him.

3) **Marta compra comida para Juana.**
   _____

   Marta buys food for Juana.
   Marta buys it for her.

4) **Ellos regalan el dinero a ellas.**
   _____

   They give the money to them.
   They give it to them.

5) **Elena le cuenta la historia a Marco.**
   _____

   Elena tells the history to Marco.
   Elena tells it to him.

6) **Ellos me dan los tacos.**
   _____

   They give me the tacos.
   They give them to me.

7) **Juana te escribe la carta.**
   _____

   Juana writes you a letter.
   Juana writes it to you.

8) **Julia me compra el carro.**
   _____

   Julia buys me the car.
   Julia buys it for me.

9) **Te doy los datos.**
   _____

   I am giving you the data.
   I am giving it to you.

10) **Les doy los pasaportes.**
    _____

    I give them the passports.
    I give them to them.

ANSWERS TO PRACTICE: OBJECT PRONOUNS: PEOPLE & THINGS

Level 1: Fill in the blanks with **me**, **te**, **le**, **nos**, or **les**. Use the sentence in English as a guide.

1. me
2. le
3. te
4. les
5. nos
6. les
7. me
8. te
9. les
10. le
11. me
12. le
13. me
14. nos
15. nos

Level 2: Substitute the **direct object** with a **direct object pronoun** (**lo**, **la**, **los**, **las**).

1. las
2. lo
3. la
4. los
5. lo
6. los
7. la
8. las
9. las
10. la

Level 2: Replace the underlined **direct objects** in the question with **direct object pronouns** in the answer. Use **DOP**'s in your responses (**lo**, **la**, **los**, **las**).

1. Sí, la como.
2. No, no lo bebo mucho.
3. Sí, los comen.
4. No, no las compra.
5. Sí, los leen.
6. No, no las escribo.
7. Sí, la tengo.
8. Sí, lo veo.
9. Sí, las quiero comer.
10. Sí, lo quiero cocinar.

Level 3: Read the questions carefully, then answer with **me**, **te**, **le**, **nos**, or **les**.

1. No, Raúl no nos vende el libro.
2. Sí, les compro la cena.
3. Sí, me dan el dinero.
4. Sí, les hacemos desayuno.
5. Sí, me dan la llanta.
6. Sí, les compro las bebidas.
7. No, no nos dicen nada.

Level 3: Substitute both the **direct objects** and **indirect objects** with **double object pronouns**.

1. Juan se lo da a ella.
2. Lalo se lo dice a él.
3. Marta se la compra para ella.
4. Ellos se lo dan a ellas.
5. Elena se la cuenta a él.
6. Ellos me los dan.
7. Juana te la escribe.
8. Julia me lo compra.
9. Te los doy.
10. Se los doy.

Hand Tools

THERE IS / THERE ARE: HAY

Hay un hotel.
There is a hotel.

No hay un hotel.
There is not a hotel.

Hay (pronounced "eye") is a form of the verb **haber**. **Hay** means *there is* or *there are*. **Hay** is indispensible for describing, or asking yes-or-no questions about a location. **Hay** is used to tell if something is present or absent.

TELLING WHAT IS PRESENT OR ABSENT

Hay playas buenas.	*There are good beaches.*
Hay un perro en el jardín.	*There is a dog in the yard.*
No hay una playa aquí.	*There is not a beach here.*
Hay cuartos disponibles.	*There are rooms available.*
No hay un banco abierto.	*There is not a bank open.*

ASKING YES-OR-NO QUESTIONS ABOUT WHAT IS PRESENT

¿Hay playas buenas?	*Are there good beaches?*
¿Hay una vista?	*Is there a view?*
¿Hay vuelos a San Diego?	*Are there flights to San Diego?*
¿Hay pollo en el menú?	*Is there chicken on the menu?*
¿Hay cuartos disponibles?	*Are there rooms available?*

Hand Tools

THERE IS / THERE ARE: HAY

CONVERSATION

Jeff asks Julieta about Cancún. He wants to know what to expect if he were to visit.

Jeff: ¿Cómo es Cancún? ¿Qué **hay** en Cancún? ¿Es un buen lugar para visitar?

What is Cancun like? What **is there** in Cancun? Is it a good place to visit?

Julieta: Cancún es divertidísimo. **Hay** ruinas. **Hay** playas hermosas. Y claro, **hay** hoteles fabulosos.

Cancun is really fun. **There are** ruins. **There are** beautiful beaches. And of course, **there are** fabulous hotels.

Jeff: Quiero quedarme en un hotel que tenga vista al mar. **Hay** unos hoteles en la playa me imagino.

I want to stay in a hotel that has a view of the ocean. **There are** some hotels on the beach I imagine.

Julieta: Sí, **hay** muchos hoteles en la playa en Cancún. **Hay** hoteles en las afueras de Cancún. También, **hay** hoteles muy retirados si quieres esconderte un poco.

Yes, **there are** a lot of hotels on the beach in Cancun. **There are** hotels on the outskirts of Cancun. Also, **there are** hotels a long way away if you want to hide out a bit.

Jeff: Bien, me suena que **hay** muchas posibilidades. **Hay** un montón de opciones.

Good, it sounds like **there are** a lot of possibilities. **There are** a ton of options.

Julieta: Jeffcito, tienes que investigar un poco más. Busca en el Internet. **Hay** mucho que ver.

Jeffy, you have to investigate a little more. Look on the Internet. **There is** a lot to see.

Hand Tools

 PRACTICE LEVEL 1: HAY

DIRECTIONS: Insert **hay** to complete each sentence.

1. _____ museos en el parque.	*There are* museums in the park.
2. _____ pollo en el menú.	*There is* chicken on the menu.
3. _____ peces en el mar.	*There are* fish in the sea.
5. No _____ un vuelo temprano.	*There is* not an early flight.
6. _____ libros en inglés.	*There are* books in English.
7. No _____ dos hoteles aquí.	*There are* not two hotels here.
8. _____ una cantina cerca.	*There is* a cantina close.
9. _____ un montón de ganado.	*There is* a bunch of cattle.
10. _____ gente allí.	*There are* people there.

PRACTICE LEVEL 2: HAY

DIRECTIONS: Use **hay** to ask questions.

11. ¿_____?	*Are there two bicycles?*
12. ¿_____?	*Is there a dog in the house?*
13. ¿_____?	*Are there towels in the room?*
14. ¿_____?	*Is there a taxi at the hotel?*
15. ¿_____?	*Are there ruins in Xochitlán?*
16. ¿_____?	*Is there more wine?*
17. ¿_____?	*Is there a restaurant in the airport?*
18. ¿_____?	*Are there many options?*
19. ¿_____?	*Are there waves?*
20. ¿_____?	*Is there another menú?*

ANSWERS TO PRACTICE: HAY

Level 1: Insert **hay** to complete each sentence.

1. hay
2. hay
3. hay
4. hay
5. hay
6. hay
7. hay
8. hay
9. hay
10. hay

Level 2: Use **hay** to ask questions.

11. ¿Hay dos bicicletas?
12. ¿Hay un perro en la casa?
13. ¿Hay toallas en el cuarto?
14. ¿Hay un taxi en el hotel?
15. ¿Hay ruinas en Xochitlán?
16. ¿Hay más vino?
17. ¿Hay un restaurante en el aeropuerto?
18. ¿Hay muchas opciones?
19. ¿Hay olas?
20. ¿Hay otro menú?

SECTION 3

NUTS & BOLTS
CHAPTERS 9-12

Nuts & Bolts

SAYING…	TITLE	TOOL	PAGE
9. *Speak Spanish! Don't speak English!*	Instruction & Suggestion: Commands	**Positive and negative commands: tú, ud., nosotros, uds.**	67
10. *Actions you do to yourself*	Reflexive Verbs	**Verbs that end in se… llamarse, despertarse**	74
11. *I know ___*	To Know	**Saber & Conocer**	78
12. *Speaking about the past*	The Past Tenses	**Preterite & Imperfect**	81

Nuts & Bolts

INSTRUCTION & SUGGESTION: COMMANDS

USTED
commands

Hable usted español.
No hable usted inglés.
Speak Spanish.
Don't speak English.

TÚ
commands

Habla tú español.
No hables tú inglés.
Speak Spanish.
Don't speak English.

Commands can be **positive** *(eat)* or **negative** *(don't eat)*. Commands can occur in **tú**, **usted**, **nosotros**, **ustedes**, and ***vosotros*** forms.[1]

Positive tú commands are formed one way, while all other commands are formed in another way. There are also some **irregular command** forms.

POSITIVE TÚ COMMANDS (EAT!)

🔑 Most **positive tú commands** are identical to the **él**, **ella**, and **usted** form, in the present tense (there are a handful of irregular verbs that do not follow this pattern, they are listed later).

	CORRER	ESCRIBIR	HABLAR
yo	_____	_____	_____
tú	_____	_____	_____
él, ella, usted	corre	escribe	habla
nosotros	_____	_____	_____
vosotros	_____	_____	_____
ustedes, ellos	_____	_____	_____

The he/she form is the positive tú command.

¡Corre a casa!	*Run home!*
Escribe una carta.	*Write a letter.*
Habla más fuerte.	*Speak louder.*

---

1   ***Vosotros*** commands will not be treated in this book.

Nuts & Bolts

NEGATIVE TÚ COMMANDS (DON'T EAT!)

All negative commands have **no** in front of the verb: **no hables** (*don't speak*), **no comas** (*don't eat*). ✎ To form most negative **tú** commands, conjugate a verb to the **yo** form in the present tense, take off the **-o**, and add the opposite present tense ending. **ER/IR** verbs take the **AR** verb ending (**-as**). **AR** verbs take **ER/IR** the ending (**-es**).

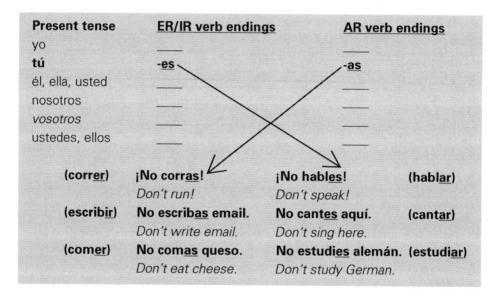

Present tense	ER/IR verb endings	AR verb endings
yo	____	____
tú	-es	-as
él, ella, usted	____	____
nosotros	____	____
vosotros	____	____
ustedes, ellos	____	____

(correr)	¡No corras!	¡No hables!	(hablar)
	Don't run!	*Don't speak!*	
(escribir)	No escribas email.	No cantes aquí.	(cantar)
	Don't write email.	*Don't sing here.*	
(comer)	No comas queso.	No estudies alemán.	(estudiar)
	Don't eat cheese.	*Don't study German.*	

IRREGULAR TÚ COMMANDS

Below is a list of common **irregular tú commands**. The **negative** counterparts of the **irregular tú commands** are the same as the **subjunctive form**.

infinitive	positive tú	negative tú	
DECIR	di	no digas	*to say or tell*
IR	ve	no vayas	*to go*
PONER	pon	no pongas	*to put or place*
SER	sé	no seas	*to be*
VENIR	ven	no vengas	*to come*
HACER	haz	no hagas	*to do or make*
SALIR	sal	no salgas	*to leave*
TENER	ten	no tengas	*to have*
VER	ve	no veas	*to see*

Nuts & Bolts

USTED AND USTEDES COMMANDS

Positive and **negative usted (Ud.)** and **ustedes (Uds.) commands** are created in the same way as a negative **tú** command. Change the verb to the **yo** form, take off the -**o**, and add the opposite present tense ending. **ER/IR** verbs take **AR** endings (-**a** or -**an**). **AR** verbs take **ER/IR** endings (-**e** or -**en**).

	CORRER	**ESCRIBIR**	**HABLAR**
Ud.	corra	escriba	hable
Uds.	corran	escriban	hablen

¡Corra Ud.!	No escriba Ud. email.	Hable español por favor.
¡Corran Uds.!	No escriban Uds. email.	Hablen español por favor.
Run!	*Don't write email.*	*Please speak Spanish.*

IRREGULAR USTED AND USTEDES COMMANDS

Similar to the negative **tú commands**, verbs that end in -**car**, -**gar**, and -**zar**, are **irregular in the Ud. and Uds. commands**.

TOCAR	toque / toquen	*to touch or play an instrument*
JUGAR	juegue / jueguen	*to play*
EMPEZAR	empiece / empiecen	*to start or begin*

There are a few common verbs that have irregular **Ud**. and **Uds**. commands.

DAR	dé / den	*to give*
ESTAR	esté / estén	*to be*
IR	vaya / vayan	*to go*
SABER	sepa / sepan	*to know*
SER	sea / sean	*to be*

NOSOTROS COMMANDS

Nosotros commands are formed using the *opposite* endings, and are identical to the **nosotros subjunctive** form (with the exception of the positive **ir**, **¡vamos!**). In English, the **nosotros commands** translate to *let's..!, let's go!, let's leave!, let's party!*

¡Corramos!	*Let's run!*
¡Escribamos postales!	*Let's write post cards!*
¡Hablemos español!	*Let's speak Spanish!*

When a **reflexive verb** is used in a **positive nosotros command**, the final **s** is dropped before the attached pronoun.

¡Vámonos ya!	*Let's go already!*
¡Llamámonos más!	*Let's call each other more!*

COMMANDS WITH OBJECT PRONOUNS

POSITIVE AND NEGATIVE COMMANDS

When using an **object pronoun** with a command, the **pronoun** goes in front of negative commands, and is connected to the end of positive commands.

Di<u>me</u>.	*Tell me.*
No <u>me</u> digas.	*Don't tell me.*

ACCENTS

When a command with an attached **pronoun** (or pronouns) has three or more syllables, an accent is placed on the stressed syllable.

Dímelo.	*Tell it to me.*
Cómpralo.	*Buy it.*

ORDER OF TWO PRONOUNS TOGETHER

Notice that when both **indirect** and **direct object pronouns** are used in a command, they are always presented **indirect** first, and **direct** second ("**ID**"). The pronouns are never separated.

Cocí<u>name</u>la, por favor.	*Cook it for me, please.*
No <u>me la</u> cocines.	*Don't cook it for me.*

Nuts & Bolts

 EXERCISES: TÚ, USTED, USTEDES, AND NOSOTROS COMMANDS

Fill in each blank with a **tú command**.

1. _____ las enchiladas. (comer)	*Eat the enchiladas.*
2. No _____ el pollo. (cocinar)	*Don't cook the chicken.*
3. _____ con la señora. (hablar)	*Speak with the lady.*
4. No _____ fuerte. (cantar)	*Don't sing loudly.*
5. _____ el regalo. (comprar)	*Buy the gift.*
6. _____ la verdad. (decir)	*Tell the truth.*
7. No _____ las ruinas. (visitar)	*Don't visit the ruins.*
8. _____ aquí. (venir)	*Come here.*
9. No _____ tan lento. (correr)	*Don't run so slow.*
10. No _____ una carta. (escribir)	*Don't write a letter.*

Fill in the blanks with **usted commands**.

11. _____ aquí. (ver)	*Look, here.*
12. No _____ el vaso. (romper)	*Don't break the glass.*
13. _____ el cliente. (buscar)	*Look for the client.*
14. No _____ tan lejos. (ir)	*Don't go so far.*
15. _____ todo el libro. (leer)	*Read the whole book.*
16. _____ la mesa, por favor. (poner)	*Set the table, please.*
17. No _____ el puerco. (comer)	*Don't eat the pork.*
18. _____ la carta. (mandar)	*Send the letter.*
19. No _____ a mi casa. (venir)	*Don't come to my house.*
20. No _____ los shorts. (llevar)	*Don't wear shorts.*

Use **ustedes commands** in the blanks below.

21. No _____ **de la casa. (salir)**	*Don't leave the house.*
22. No _____ **tanto. (estudiar)**	*Don't study so much.*
23. _____ **el dinero aquí. (dejar)**	*Leave the money here.*
24. No _____ **tan lejos. (ir)**	*Don't go so far.*
25. _____ **todo el libro. (leer)**	*Read the whole book.*
26. _____ **la mesa, por favor. (poner)**	*Set the table, please.*
27. No _____ **el puerco. (comer)**	*Don't eat the pork.*
28. _____ **la carta. (mandar)**	*Send the letter.*
29. _____ **a mi casa. (venir)**	*Come to my house.*
30. No _____ **los shorts. (llevar)**	*Don't wear shorts.*

Insert **nosotros commands.**

31. _____ **en la playa. (correr)**	*Let's run on the beach.*
32. No _____ **Guatemala. (visitar)**	*Let's not visit Guatemala.*
33. _____ **hamacas. (comprar)**	*Let's buy hammocks.*
34. ¡ _____ **ya! (comer)**	*Let's eat already!*
35. _____ **, a las seis. (decir)**	*Let's say, at six.*

Nuts & Bolts

 ANSWERS TO EXERCISES

Fill in each blank with a **tú command**.

1. come
2. cocines
3. habla
4. cantes
5. compra
6. di
7. visites
8. ven
9. corras
10. escribas

Fill in the blanks with **usted commands**.

11. vea
12. rompa
13. busque
14. vaya
15. lea
16. ponga
17. coma
18. mande
19. venga
20. lleve

Use **ustedes commands** in the blanks below.

21. salgan
22. estudien
23. dejen
24. vayan
25. lean
26. pongan
27. coman
28. manden
29. vengan
30. lleven

Insert **Nosotros commands**.

31. corramos
32. visitemos
33. compremos
34. comamos
35. digamos

REFLEXIVE VERBS

Reflexive verbs end in -**se** in the infinitive form (**lavarse, acostarse, sentarse**). Reflexive verbs are associated with actions you *do to yourself*, such as combing your hair, or brushing your teeth. For example, the reflexive **lavarse** means *to wash yourself*, while **lavar**, means *to wash*. Reflexive verbs must be used with a reflexive pronoun (**me, te, se, nos, *os*, se**).

Me lavo.
I wash myself. (reflexive)

Lavo el perro.
I wash the dog. (non-reflexive)

LAVARSE

me lavo
te lavas
se lava
nos lavamos
os laváis
se lavan

When using reflexive verbs, conjugate normally, and always use the matching pronoun: **me** is always used with the **yo** ending (**me lavo**), **te** is always used with the **tú** ending (**te lavas**), etc. Below, **lavarse** is conjugated normally, and the corresponding pronoun is used in each sentence.

me lavo	**Me quiero lavar la cara ya.**
	I want to wash my face already.
te lavas	**Te lavas temprano.**
	You wash yourself early.
se lava	**Rolo se lava por la noche.**
	Rolo washes (himself) at night.
nos lavamos	**Nos lavamos diario.**
	We wash (ourselves) daily.
se lavan	**Se lavan las manos muy bien.**
	They wash their hands well.

PLACING PRONOUNS IN SENTENCES

Reflexive pronouns follow the same rules for placement as other object pronouns. There are three possible positions on the following page.

Nuts & Bolts

BEFORE A CONJUGATED VERB

Me lavo el cabello por la mañana.	*I wash my hair in the morning.*
Ella se seca rápidamente.	*She dries herself qucikly.*

ATTACHED TO THE INFINITIVE

Quiero despertarme a las seis.	*I want to wake up at six.*
Necesitan dormirse pronto.	*They need to fall asleep soon.*

ATTACHED TO THE "-ING" ENDING

*this placement requires an accent on the stressed syllable

Estoy lavándome las manos ahora.	*I am washing my hands now.*
Estás mirándote mucho.	*You are looking at yourself a lot.*

A list of reflexive verbs follows. They are listed in the infinitive form, and conjugated to the **yo** form.

INFINITIVE	YO FORM	TRANSLATION
acostarse (ue)	me acuesto	I go to bed
afeitarse	me afeito	I shave
bañarse	me baño	I bathe
cepillarse los dientes	me cepillo los dientes	I brush my teeth
despertarse (ie)	me despierto	I wake up
divertirse (ie)	me divierto	I enjoy myself/have a good time
dormirse (ue)	me duermo	I fall asleep
ducharse	me ducho	I shower
lavarse el pelo	me lavo el pelo	I wash my hair
levantarse	me levanto	I get up
llamarse	me llamo	I call myself (my name is)
maquillarse	me maquillo	I put on makeup
peinarse	me peino	I comb my hair
ponerse la ropa (irreg)	me pongo la ropa	I put on my clothes
quitarse la ropa	me quito la ropa	I take off my clothes
secarse	me seco	I dry myself
sentarse (ie)	me siento	I sit down
vestirse (i)	me visto	I dress myself

EXERCISES: REFLEXIVE VERBS

Conjuagate the reflexive verbs, and use the correct pronoun in each sentence.

1. Ellos _____ temprano. (levantarse)   *They get up early.*
2. Yo _____ todos los días. (ducharse)   *I shower every day.*
3. El _____ Eduardo. (llamarse)   *His name is Eduardo. (He calls himself Eduardo.)*
4. José _____ por la mañana. (bañarse)   *Jose bathes in the morning.*
5. Los niños _____ los dientes. (cepillarse)   *The children brush their teeth.*
6. Tú siempre _____ ese abrigo. (ponerse)   *You always put on that coat.*
7. Yo _____ en seguida. (dormirse)   *I fall asleep right away.*
8. Nosotros _____ a las seis. (acostarse)   *We go to bed at six.*
9. Yo _____ bien en el trabajo. (vestirse)   *I dress well at work.*
10. Samuel no _____ la gorra. (quitarse)   *Samuel does not take off the hat.*
11. Ellos _____ muy tarde. (despertarse)   *They wake up very late.*
12. Tú _____ aquí. (divertirse)   *You have a good time here.*

Nuts & Bolts

 ANSWERS TO EXECISES

Conjuagate the reflexive verbs, and use the correct pronoun in each sentence.

1. se levantan
2. me ducho
3. se llama
4. se baña
5. se cepillan
6. te pones
7. me duermo
8. nos acostamos
9. me visto
10. se quita
11. se despiertan
12. te diviertes

TO KNOW: SABER & CONOCER

Both **saber** and **conocer** mean *to know*. But, they have distinct uses…

SABER is related to facts or information in your HEAD.

CONOCER is for people you know and places you have touched with your HAND.

SABER – *to know*	**CONOCER** – *to know*
sé	conozco
sabes	conoces
sabe	conoce
sabemos	conocemos
sabéis	*conocéis*
saben	conocen

SABER…the head

Ella sabe hablar español.
She knows how to speak Spanish.

Yo sé mucho de la geografía.
I know a lot about geography.

José sabe que hay un camino.
José knows there is a road.

Tú no sabes quien es Juan.
You don't know who Juan is.

CONOCER…the hand

Conozco a Lalo y a Eduardo.
I know Lalo and Eduardo.

Ed conoce Taxco.
Ed knows Taxco (he has been there).

Yo conozco el camino.
I know the road (I have traveled it).

Ellos conocen a Juan.
They know Juan.

Nuts & Bolts

 EXERCISES: TO KNOW: SABER & CONOCER

Fill in the blanks with a form of **saber**.

1. ¿ Tú _____ quién es el presidente?
   Do you know who is the president?

2. Juan _____ jugar béisbol.
   Juan knows how to play baseball.

3. Yo no _____ el número.
   I don't know the number.

4. Nosotros _____ la respuesta.
   We all know the answer.

5. ¿Tú _____ la ruta al capital?
   Do you know the route to the capital?

Use a form of **conocer** below.

6. Yo _____ bien a Xuxa.
   I know Xuxa quite well.

7. No _____ Chile.
   You don't know (haven't been to) Chile.

8. Ellos _____ el camino sureño.
   They know the southern route.

9. Yo _____ a toda la familia.
   I know the whole family.

10. Juanito _____ Punta Chivato.
    Juanito knows (has been to) Punta Chivato.

Use a form or either **saber** or **conocer**.

11. Ellos _____ a la mamá de ella.
    They know her mother.

12. Carmen _____ mi casa.
    Carmen knows (has been to) my house.

13. Yo _____ a la maestra.
    I know the teacher.

14. Nosotros _____ escribir.
    We know how to write.

15. Tú _____ la dirección.
    You know the address.

Nuts & Bolts

 ANSWERS TO EXERCISES

Fill in the blanks with a form of **saber**.

1. sabes
2. sabe
3. sé
4. sabemos
5. sabes

Use a form of **conocer** below.

6. conozco
7. conoces
8. conocen
9. conozco
10. conoce

Use a form or either **saber** or **conocer**.

11. conocen
12. conoce
13. conozco
14. sabemos
15. sabes

Nuts & Bolts

PAST TENSES: PRETERITE & IMPERFECT

There are two common past tenses, the **preterite**, and the **imperfect**. Both are used to describe something that occurred in the past. In general, when the speaker uses the **preterite**, he/she is focusing on <u>a specific moment in time</u>. The **imperfect** describes <u>ongoing or recurring actions, events, feelings, etc</u>.

The <u>preterite</u> occurs in an instant.

I <u>bought</u> the car.

The <u>imperfect</u> takes more time.

I <u>was</u> in love.

EVENTS AND ACTIONS

The **imperfect** describes events and actions that take place over time (the boys <u>were talking</u>, she <u>was studying</u>). The **preterite** emphasizes a specific moment in the past: an action that began, ended, or was completed (the boys <u>started talking</u>, the car <u>crashed</u>, we <u>cooked</u> the shrimp).

Imagine tuning in to your favorite television program after it had already begun. If an activity or event were already going on when you tuned in, use the **imperfect** to describe it. If an event or action started or stopped as you watched the program, use the **preterite**.

Junior y Pablo hablaban.
Junior and Pablo were talking.

Minutos después, llegó Miguel al taller.
Minutes later, Miguel arrived at the shop.

Nuts & Bolts

CONDITIONS, MENTAL STATES

Conditions (like being sick), or mental states (like being sad) are most often described with the **imperfect**.

> **Ella <u>estaba</u> deprimida.**
> *She <u>was</u> depressed.*
> **Me <u>enojaba</u> verla.**
> *It <u>angered me</u> to see her. (I would see her with some frequency)*

If the speaker wants to emphasize that the condition or state no longer exists, the **preterite** is used.

> **Yo <u>estuve</u> enfermo.**
> *I <u>was</u> sick. (and am no longer sick)*
> **Ella <u>estuvo</u> deprimida.**
> *She <u>was</u> depressed. (and is no longer depressed)*

If a **personal reaction** to an event in the past is recounted, the **preterite** is used. In this instance, the **preterite** reflects how somebody feels at a particular moment.

> **Al verla, <u>me enojé</u>.**
> *Upon seeing her, I became angry. (describing a reaction to seeing her at a particular moment)*
> **Encontré mi cartera, y <u>me sentí</u> aliviado.**
> *I found my wallet, and <u>I felt</u> relieved.*

Nuts & Bolts

RECURRING VERSUS ONE-TIME ACTIONS OR EVENTS

RECURRING ACTIONS OR EVENTS

Actions repeated many times in the past require the **imperfect**. If you did something regularly in the past and want to refer to it, use the **imperfect**. These sentences often translate to *used to...* or *would...* (i.e., *we used to play football at school*, or *we would walk to school*).

> **_Íbamos_ a la playa todos los sábados.**
> *We used to go to the beach every Saturday.*
> **Comíamos debajo de ese árbol.**
> *We would eat under that tree.*
> **Gerardo tenía suerte en los negocios.**
> *Gerardo had luck in business. (over a period of time)*

ONE-TIME EVENTS

If a speaker wants to refer to an action that occurred one time, the **preterite** should be used. If the action or event never occurred, the **preterite** is also used.

> **Fuimos a la playa el sábado.**
> *We went to the beach on Saturday.*
> **Gerardo firmó el contrato.**
> *Gerardo signed the contract.*
> **Jimmy nunca salió del país.**
> *Jimmy never left the country.*

EMPHASIZING A SPECIFIC PERIOD OF TIME OF AN ACTION

If the speaker is emphasizing a specific period of time that something took place, the **preterite** is used. This is similar to the speaker stressing the end of a condition or mental state, as mentioned earlier.

> **Lorenzo enseño cinco años en la universidad.**
> *Lorenzo taught for five years at the university.*
> **Yo estuve tres meses en España.**
> *I was in Spain for three months.*

Nuts & Bolts

TIME, AGE

Telling the time in the past is always done in the **imperfect**.

> **Era la una cuando llegó Juan.**
> *It was one o'clock when Juan arrived.*
> **Eran las dos cuando Marta me pidió la hora.**
> *It was two o'clock when Marta asked me the time.*

Age is communicated with the **imperfect**.[1]

> **Los abuelos tenían ochenta años cuando los vi la última vez.**
> *The grandparents were eighty years old when I last saw them.*
> **En 1970, yo tenía seis años.**
> *In 1970, I was six years old.*

SPECIAL MEANINGS IN THE PRETERITE

There are also some verbs that change meaning in the **preterite**. Notice that the **preterite** is associated with moments when something happened (*or* something that never happened).

VERB meaning	PRETERITE meaning	EXAMPLES
saber, to know information	*to find out*	**Supe la verdad.** *I found out the truth.*
conocer, to know people, and places	*to meet for the first time*	**La conocí en Brazil.** *I met her in Brazil.*
querer, to want	*to try to do something*	**Quise comer.** *I tried to eat.*
no querer, not want	*to not want to do something and then not do it*	**No quise comer.** *I didn't want to eat. (and I didn't)*

---

1   Age is told with the verb **tener** (*to have*) in Spanish. In English, we say *I am fifty years old.* In Spanish, the meaning is the same, but we are saying *I have fifty years.* A proper translation is *I am fifty years old.*

Nuts & Bolts

poder, to be able to	*to be able to do something, and then do it*	**Pude nadar.** *I was able to swim.* *(and I did it)*
no poder, not be able to	*to try to do something, and not be successful*	**No pude llamar.** *I couldn't call. (I tried but was not successful)*

FORMING THE PRETERITE

-ar verbs		-er & -ir verbs	
	HABLAR – *to speak*		**COMER** – *to eat*
-é	habl**é**	-í	com**í**
-aste	habl**aste**	-iste	com**iste**
-ó	habl**ó**	-ió	com**ió**
-amos	habl**amos**	-imos	com**imos**
-asteis	*habl**asteis***	*-isteis*	*com**isteis***
-aron	habl**aron**	-ieron	com**ieron**

Verbs ending in -**ar** and -**er** do not stem-change in the **preterite**. -**Ir** stem-changing verbs will stem-change, but only in the third person singular (*he/she*) and plural (*they, you all*). In verbs ending in -**car** (**tocar**), -**gar** (**jugar**), and -**zar** (**empezar**), there is an irregular first person spelling (**toqué, jugué, empecé**).

Some common irregular verbs in the **preterite** are listed below. They are irregular in the stem. Their endings are -**e, -iste, -o, -imos, *-isteis*, -ieron**. The verbs below are presented in the **infinitive**, and the **yo** form:

estar/estuve	**poner/puse**	**saber/supe**	**venir/vine**	**poder/pude**
querer/quise	**tener/tuve**	**haber/hube**	**andar/anduve**	

Other irregular verbs include:
DECIR, dije, dijiste, dijo, dijimos, *dijisteis*, dijeron
DAR, di, diste, dio, dimos, *disteis*, dieron
TRAER, traje, trajiste, trajo, trajimos, *trajisteis*, trajeron
HACER, hice, hiciste, hizo, hicimos, *hicisteis*, hicieron
OIR, oí, oíste, oyó, oímos, *oísteis*, oyeron
VER, vi, viste, vio, vimos, *visteis*, vieron
SER and IR, fui, fuiste, fue, fuimos, *fuisteis*, fueron

Notice that the **preterite** form of **ser** and **ir** is the same. Meaning is derived from context.

Nuts & Bolts

FORMING THE IMPERFECT

-ar verbs		-er & -ir verbs	
	HABLAR – *to speak*		**COMER** – *to eat*
-aba	hab**laba**	-ía	com**ía**
-abas	hab**labas**	-ías	com**ías**
-aba	hab**laba**	-ía	com**ía**
-ábamos	hab**lábamos**	-íamos	com**íamos**
-abais	*hab**labais***	-íais	*com**íais***
-aban	hab**laban**	-ían	com**ían**

There are only three **irregular imperfect** verbs.

SER, *to be*	**VER**, *to see*	**IR**, *to go*
era	veía	iba
eras	veías	ibas
era	veía	iba
éramos	veíamos	íbamos
erais	*veíais*	*ibais*
eran	veían	iban

Nuts & Bolts

 EXERCISES: THE PAST: PRETERITE & IMPERFECT

Fill in the blank with the correct **preterite** form of the verb given.

1. Yo _____ tacos ayer. (comer)	*I ate tacos yesterday.*
2. Ellos _____ el almuerzo. (comprar)	*They bought the lunch.*
3. José _____ una carta. (escribir)	*José wrote a letter.*
4. Nosotros _____ a la playa. (ir)	*We went to the beach.*
5. Las chicas _____ al hotel. (llegar)	*The girls arrived at the hotel.*
6. Tú le _____ a Pablo. (llamar)	*You called Pablo.*
7. Yo _____ una pizza enorme. (hacer)	*I made an enormous pizza.*
8. Lalo y yo _____ ayer. (pescar)	*Lalo and I fished yesterday.*
9. ¿Quién _____ la ensalada? (hacer)	*Who made the salad?*
10. Ustedes _____ la verdad. (decir)	*You all told the truth.*
11. Yo le _____ el secreto a él. (decir)	*I told him the secret.*
12. Yo _____ fútbol con ellos. (jugar)	*I played soccer with them.*
13. Tú _____ en la playa (nadar)	*You swam at the beach.*
14. Nosotros _____ al centro. (ir)	*We went downtown.*
15. El _____ la película. (ver)	*He saw the movie.*

Fill in the blank with the correct **imperfect** form of the verb given.

1. Yo _____ a la playa mucho. (ir)	*I used to go to the beach a lot.*
2. Ella _____ cartas. (escribir)	*She used to write letters.*
3. Nosotros _____ siempre. (hablar)	*We would talk always.*
4. Tú _____ canciones. (cantar)	*You used to sing songs.*
5. Chato _____ pollo. (cocinar)	*Chato used to cook chicken.*
6. Yo nunca _____ mi cuarto. (limpiar)	*I would never clean my room.*
7. Las chicas _____ en México. (vivir)	*The girls used to live in Mexico.*
8. Lalo _____ a las fiestas. (venir)	*Lalo would come to the parties.*
9. Ellos _____ fruta todos los días. (cortar)	*They would cut fruit all day.*
10. ¿Ustedes _____ mucho? (viajar)	*Would you all travel a lot?*
11. ¿Tú _____ San Diego? (visitar)	*You used to visit San Diego?*
12. Xuxa me _____ siempre. (llamar)	*Xuxa would always call me.*
13. Nosotros _____ cursos aquí. (tomar)	*We would take courses here.*
14. El no _____ con nadie. (hablar)	*He wouldn't talk with anyone.*
15. Yo _____ visitar Cuba. (querer)	*I always wanted to visit Cuba.*

ANSWERS FOR EXERCISES: THE PAST: PRETERITE & IMPERFECT

Fill in the blank with the correct **preterite** form of the verb given.

1. comí
2. compraron
3. escribió
4. fuimos
5. llegaron
6. llamaste
7. hice
8. pescamos
9. hizo
10. dijeron
11. dije
12. jugué
13. nadaste
14. fuimos
15. vio

Fill in the blank with the correct **imperfect** form of the verb given.

1. iba
2. escribía
3. hablábamos
4. cantabas
5. cocinaba
6. limpiaba
7. vivían
8. venía
9. cortaban
10. viajaban
11. visitabas
12. llamaba
13. tomábamos
14. hablaba
15. quería

SECTION

THE TOOL SHED
CHAPTERS 13-24

4

The Tool Shed

QUICK SECTION REFERENCE

SAYING...	TITLE	TOOL	PAGE
13. *All of the tenses*	The Essential Tenses	**Present, past, future, subjunctive, present/past perfect**	91
14. *Who? Where? When? Why?*	Asking Questions: Interrogatives	**Quién, dónde, cuándo**	102
15. Verbs that don't follow the usual pattern	Key Irregular Verbs	**Decir, estar, hacer, ir, ser, tener**	104
16. The alphabet, accents, patterns, anomalies	Pronunciation	**A-Z, adiós, jolla**	107
17. *The ___, a ___, some ___*	Making Words Match	**Gender & Number**	111
18. *Mine, yours, his, hers, etc.*	Possession	**Possessive Pronouns & Adjectives**	117
19. Asking the time, telling the time, events, ___ ago	Telling Time	**Son las, es la, hace ___ que**	121
20. *This & These, That & Those*	Demonstrative Adjectives & Pronouns	**Este/esta, ese/esa, aquel/aquella**	129
21. *Bigger than, smaller than, as big as*	Comparisons	**Más ___ que, menos ___ que, tan ___ como**	128
22. *To the, of the*	Contractions	**Al & del**	129
23. *Verbs that Change in the Stem*	Stem-Changing Verbs	**Pensar, jugar, cerrar,**	132
24. *For, because of, intended for, by*	Por & Para	**Por favor, para mi amigo**	133
25. *I am ___ -ing*	Present Progressive	**Estoy hablando, estoy comiendo**	135
26. *Prices, ages, dates*	Numbers	**1, 2, 3, one thousand, two thousand**	137

The Tool Shed

THE ESSENTIAL TENSES

1) PRESENT

This is the most commonly used tense in Spanish. It is used for the following:

a) To narrate or describe something happening at the <u>present time</u>.
Escribo en inglés.
I write in English.
I am writing in English.
I do write in English.

b) *To tell a past-tense story in the present.* This is often called the <u>historical present</u>; it makes a past event sound more vivid.
Me llama y me pregunta, "¿Está Rolo en casa?"
She calls me and asks, "Is Rolo home?"

c) To talk about the <u>immediate future</u>.
Mi hermana se gradúa mañana.
My sister graduates tomorrow.

🔧 To form the **present tense** for regular verbs, drop the last two letters of the infinitive, and add the following endings.

For -**ar** verbs (**hablar**), habl<u>o</u>, habl<u>as</u>, habl<u>a</u>, habl<u>amos</u>, *habl<u>áis</u>*, habl<u>an</u>
For -**er** verbs (**comer**), com<u>o</u>, com<u>es</u>, com<u>e</u>, com<u>emos</u>, *com<u>éis</u>*, com<u>en</u>
For -**ir** verbs (**escribir**), escrib<u>o</u>, escrib<u>es</u>, escrib<u>e</u>, escrib<u>imos</u>, *escrib<u>ís</u>*, escrib<u>en</u>

2) TWO PAST TENSES

There are two simple past tenses in Spanish: the **imperfect** and the **preterite**.
🔧 **The imperfect tells us about an event that was happening, or used to happen regularly.** In English, we might say *I used to go to the beach*, or *I would study Spanish every morning.* 🔧 **The preterite is used to describe an event that occurred at one specific moment in time**; *The boat sank* or *The car broke down.*

The **imperfect** is used for the following:

a) To tell about something that was <u>done habitually or regularly.</u>
   Yo <u>pescaba</u> todos los fines de semana.
   I used to fish every weekend.
   I would fish every weekend.

b) To describe the <u>background information of a story.</u>
   <u>Hacía</u> mucho sol, el viento <u>soplaba</u> en las palmeras, y uno <u>se sentía</u> a gusto en la jamaca.
   It was sunny, the wind blew in the palms, and one felt at ease in the hammock.

c) To describe most <u>physical, mental, or emotional states</u> in the past.
   <u>Estaba</u> feliz en la clase.
   I was happy in the classroom.
   Mi padre <u>era</u> alto cuando <u>era</u> joven.
   My father was tall when he was young.
   Ella <u>tenía</u> quince años.
   She was 15 years old.

d) To tell <u>time in the past.</u>
   <u>Eran</u> las once.
   It was eleven o'clock.
   ¿Qué hora <u>era</u>?
   What time was it?

To form the **imperfect** tense for regular verbs, drop the last two letters of the infinitive, and add the following endings:

For -ar verbs (**habl<u>ar</u>**), habl**<u>aba</u>**, habl**<u>abas</u>**, habl**<u>aba</u>**, habl**<u>ábamos</u>**, *habl<u>abais</u>*, habl**<u>aban</u>**

For -er verbs (**com<u>er</u>**), com**<u>ía</u>**, com**<u>ías</u>**, com**<u>ía</u>**, com**<u>íamos</u>**, *com<u>íais</u>*, com**<u>ían</u>**

For -ir verbs (**escrib<u>ir</u>**), escrib**<u>ía</u>**, escrib**<u>ías</u>**, escrib**<u>ía</u>**, escrib**<u>íamos</u>**, *escrib<u>íais</u>*, escrib**<u>ían</u>**

There are only three irregular verbs in the **imperfect**.
Ser: era, eras, era, éramos, *erais*, eran
Ir: iba, ibas, iba, íbamos, *ibais*, iban
Ver: veía, veías, veía, veíamos, *veíais*, veían

The Tool Shed

The **preterite** is used for the following:

a) To describe <u>actions</u> that took place at <u>a specific point in time</u>.

Rompí el vaso.

> *I broke the glass.*
>
> *I did break the glass.*

Las hermanas <u>llegaron</u> ayer.

> *The sisters arrived yesterday.*

<u>Salí</u> de la casa, <u>subí</u> al carro, y <u>manejé</u> a la playa.

> *I left the house, got in the car, and drove to the beach.*

To form the **preterite** tense for regular verbs, drop the last two letters of the infinitive, and add the following endings:

For -**ar** verbs (**hablar**), habl**é**, habl**aste**, habl**ó**, habl**amos**, *habl**asteis***, habl**aron**

For -**er** verbs (**comer**), com**í**, com**iste**, com**ió**, com**imos**, *com**isteis***, com**ieron**

For -**ir** verbs (**escribir**), escrib**í**, escrib**iste**, escrib**ió**, escrib**imos**, *escrib**isteis***, escrib**ieron**

PRETERITE AND IMPERFECT TOGETHER

Both the **imperfect** and the **preterite** are sometimes used in one sentence. When this occurs, the verbs are usually presented in the form of "foreground and background." The **imperfect** is the background (describing the scene), while the **preterite** is the foreground (describing the action). The **imperfect** can be a feeling or a state of being (the background), while the **preterite** is usually an event or the focus of attention (the foreground).

<u>Había</u> poca luz en la casa cuando Bessma <u>prendió</u> la lámpara.

> *There was little light in the house when Bessma turned on the lamp.*

<u>Tenía</u> mucho sueño cuando me <u>llamó</u> Opal.

> *I was very sleepy when Opal called me.*

<u>Llegué</u> a las dos y hasta entonces todos <u>dormían</u> muy ricos.

> *I arrived at two, and up to that point, everyone was sound asleep.*

3) THE TWO FUTURES

There are two forms used to describe the future: the **future tense**, and the **informal future**.

The **future tense** is used to express <u>something that will occur in the future, or it indicates conjecture (a guess) about the present.</u>

a) To describe <u>an occurance in the future</u>.
   Escribirán la carta mañana.
   They will write the letter tomorrow.
   Cocinaremos el pavo el martes.
   We will cook the turkey on Tuesday.

b) To describe <u>conjecture about the present</u>.
   ¿Habrá cupo?
   Is there room?
   Tendrán una casa llena.
   They probably have a full house.

🔑 For the regular verbs, the **future** is formed by adding -**é**, -**ás**, -**á**, -**emos**, -*éis*, -**án** to the end of the **infinitive**.

hablar: hablar**é**, hablar**ás**, hablar**á**, hablar**emos,** *hablaréis*, hablar**án**
comer: comer**é**, comer**ás**, comer**á**, comer**emos**, *comeréis*, comer**án**
escribir: escribir**é**, escribir**ás**, escribir**á**, escribir**emos**, *escribiréis*, escribir**án**

The **informal future** (although not a tense) is primarily used when speaking about an event in the future. 🔑 The **informal future** is created with the formula: **Ir + a + infinitive**, and is translated as *going to...* The present tense forms of **ir** are **voy**, **vas**, **va**, **vamos**, *vais*, **van**.

<u>**Voy a hacer**</u> un cóctel de camarones.
   I am going to make a shrimp cocktail.
<u>**Van a comprar**</u> ropa.
   They are going to buy clothing.
<u>**Vamos a visitar**</u> a Mikkel en Dinamarca.
   We are going to visit Mikkel in Denmark.

The Tool Shed

4) THE CONDITIONAL

The **conditional** usually expresses <u>would</u>. Such as *I <u>would</u> eat*, or *They <u>would</u> buy a ticket.*

---

a) The **conditional** often suggests <u>a feeling of longing or desire</u>.
   Me <u>encantaría</u> más ceviche.
   I would love more ceviche.
   En un día como hoy, yo <u>pescaría</u>.
   On a day like today, I would go fishing.

b) It is often used <u>with the **past subjunctive** to express something someone would do, if something else were possible</u>.
   Yo <u>compraría</u> una casa si tuviera más dinero.
   I would buy a house, if I had money.
   Juana <u>iría</u> a París si ganara la loteria.
   Juana would go to Paris if she won the lottery.

🔑 The **conditional** is formed by adding the endings below to the infinitive form of a verb. There are several irregular forms of the **conditional**; these are the same verbs that are irregular in the **future tense**.

hablar: hablar**ía**, hablar**ías**, hablar**ía**, hablar**íamos**, *hablar**íais***, hablar**ían**

5) PRESENT SUBJUNCTIVE

The **subjunctive** is a *mood*. The **subjunctive** usually occurs in sentences with two verbs, and a conjunction like **que** separating the verbs. The **subjunctive** occurs in the second verb. It expresses the following:

---

a) <u>A wish or desire</u>, often with the purpose of getting someone else to do something.
   Quiero que <u>vengas</u> a la fiesta.
   I want you to come to the party.
   Insisto que <u>comas</u> en el patio.
   I insist that you eat on the patio.
   Prefieren que <u>lleguemos</u> pronto.
   They prefer we arrive soon.

---

b) <u>doubt or uncertainty</u>.

Dudo que <u>haya</u> gente en la casa.

I doubt that there are people in the house.

No conozco a nadie que <u>pueda</u> ayudarnos.

I don't know anyone who can help us.

Busco a alguien que <u>tenga</u> un carro parecido.

I am looking for someone that has a similar car.

c) <u>a possible outcome, given that certain conditions are met</u>. It often suggests uncertainty. The **future tense** is often used as one of the verbs in the sentence, and one of the following conjunctions are often present: **antes (de) que, cuando, después (de) que, hasta que, mientras, con tal de que, para que, a fin de que, en caso de que,** and **sin que**. The **present subjunctive** is not used, however, if the first verb in the sentence is in the past, or if the sentence suggests a habitual action.[1]

Voy a comprar una casa cuando <u>tenga</u> dinero.

I am going to buy a house when I have money.

Hablaré con la esposa con tal de que la carta <u>llegue</u> mañana.

I will talk with my wife provided that the letter arrives tomorrow.

Te llamaré cuando ella me <u>llame</u> a mí.

I will call you, when she calls me.

d) <u>a personal opinion expressing necessity, doubt, regret, or urgency</u>. These sentences often begin with the following phrases: **es necesario, es preciso, es urgente, no creo, temo,** and **espero**. Or, their negative, **no es necesario, no es preciso**, etc.[2]

Es necesario que ellos <u>trabajen</u> duro.

It's necessary that they work hard.

Temo que ya se <u>hayan</u> ido.

I'm afraid they have already gone.

Esperan que yo <u>llame</u> a tiempo.

They hope that I call on time.

---

1   This would include **Remé hasta que no pude** (*I rowed until I couldn't any longer*). And, **Gasto dinero cuando lo tengo**.(*I spend money when I have it*).

2   Even though **no creo** requires the subjunctive, the positive **creo** does not. **No creo** suggests doubt, while **creo** indicates certainty when used in Spanish.

The Tool Shed

e) after **ojalá** (meaning *I hope* or *I wish*).

Ojalá que Luisa <u>esté</u> en casa.

I hope that Luisa is at home.

Ojalá que la obra <u>termine</u> pronto.

I hope the play ends soon.

The **present subjunctive** is formed as follows. Drop the **-o** from the present indicative **yo** form of a verb, and then put on the following endings:

For **-ar** verbs (**habl<u>ar</u>**), habl**<u>e</u>**, habl**<u>es</u>**, habl**<u>e</u>**, habl**<u>emos</u>**, *habl<u>éis</u>*, habl**<u>en</u>**

For **-er** verbs (**com<u>er</u>**), com**<u>a</u>**, com**<u>as</u>**, com**<u>a</u>**, com**<u>amos</u>**, *com<u>áis</u>*, com**<u>an</u>**

For **-ir** verbs (**escrib<u>ir</u>**), escrib**<u>a</u>**, escrib**<u>as</u>**, escrib**<u>a</u>**, escrib**<u>amos</u>**, *escrb<u>áis</u>*, escrib**<u>an</u>**

6) PAST SUBJUNCTIVE

The **past subjunctive** is used similarly to the present subjunctive.

a) <u>to express doubt, uncertainty, desire, and opinion</u>. The verb in the main clause, however, must be in the past, or conditional.

Yo quería que las gemelas <u>vinieran</u> juntas.

I wanted the twins to come together.

Supliqué que <u>hablaran</u> menos fuerte.

I begged them to speak less loudly.

Ella me habló para que le <u>dijera</u> más.

She called me so that I would tell her more.

b) <u>to express ideas that are contrary to fact</u>. These sentences use **como si** (*as if*) or **si** (*if*). In sentences with **si**, the conditional is often used in addition to the past subjunctive.

Lola gasta dinero como <u>si fuera</u> rica.

Lola spends money as if she were rich.

Marcos habla como <u>si tuviera</u> un puesto en el gobierno.

Marcos talks as if he had a job in the government.

Marcos talks like he had a job in the government.

<u>Si tuviera</u> un barco, pescaría más.

If I had a boat, I would fish more.

Nadaría todos los días <u>si viviera</u> en la playa.

I would swim every day if I lived at the beach.

🔧 To form the **past subjunctive** of any verb, take the third person plural form of the **preterite**, drop the -**on** ending, and add the endings -**a, -as, -a, -amos, -ais, -an**. An accent is placed on the vowel preceeding the **nosotros** ending.

~~hablaron~~ becomes hablar**a**, hablar**as**, hablar**a**, hablár**amos**, *hablarais*, hablar**an**

~~comieron~~ becomes comier**a**, comier**as**, comier**a**, comiér**amos**, *comierais*, comier**an**

~~escribieron~~ becomes escribier**a**, escribier**as**, escribier**a**, escribiér**amos**, *escribierais*, escribier**an**

7) PRESENT PERFECT

The **present perfect** conveys <u>has/have happened</u>, such as *I have done the work*. It is constructed with a form of **haber** in the present tense, together with the **past participle** (*spoken, opened, broken*). The **present perfect** can also occur in the **subjunctive** mood. It is used under the same circumstances as the present **subjunctive** (used to express doubt, uncertainty, personal opinion, and so forth). When the **past participle** is used in the **present perfect** construction, it does not change for **gender** or **number**.

a) The **present perfect indicative** uses a form of haber in the present tense indicative (**he, has, ha, hemos, *habéis*, han**) and the past participle.
> Yo <u>he intentando</u> mil veces.
>> *I have tried a thousand times.*
> Eddie <u>ha comido</u> el almuerzo ya.
>> *Eddie has eaten lunch already.*

b) The **present perfect subjunctive** uses a form of **haber** in the **present subjunctive** (**haya, hayas, haya, hayamos, *hayáis*, hayan**) and follows other general **subjunctive** rules.
> Dudo que <u>hayan llegado</u>.
>> *I doubt they have arrived.*
> Es posible que ella <u>haya hecho</u> la tarea.
>> *It is possible that she has done the homework.*

The Tool Shed

8) PAST PERFECT

a) The **past perfect** conveys what <u>had happened</u>, such as *Juan had purchased the house.* This tense is constructed with the **imperfect** (past) of **haber** and the **past participle**.

Natalia <u>había ido</u> ya.
Natalia had gone already.

Ellos <u>habían pagado</u> la cuenta.
They had paid the bill.

b) The **past perfect** is often used <u>to describe an action that took place before another action</u>.

Ya <u>habían llegado</u> cuando llegué yo.
They had already arrived when I arrived.

Llamé a la casa, pero ya <u>habían salido</u>.
I called the house, but they had already left.

c) Other **perfect tenses** in the past include the **preterite perfect**, and the **past perfect subjunctive**. They are also formed with their respective forms of **haber**, and the **past particple**.

Haber is conjugated as follows:
Present: **he, has, ha, hemos, *habéis*, han**
Imperfect: **había, habías, había, habíamos, *hubierais*, habían**
Present Subjunctive: **haya, hayas, haya, hayamos, *hayáis*, hayan**
Imperfect Subjunctive: **hubiera, hubieras, hubiera, hubiéramos, *hubierais*, hubieran**

9) PAST PARTICIPLE

The **past participle** *(spoken, eaten, measured)* ends in **-ado** for verbs ending in **-ar**, and **-ido** for verbs ending in **-er** and **-ir**. It does not change for **gender** or **number**. For example:

hablar – hablado
comer – comido
medir – medido

a) The **past participle** can be used as an **adjective** with and without the verb **estar**. When the past **participle** is used as an **adjective**, it changes for **gender** and **number**.

> With **estar**
>> **El vaso está <u>roto</u>.**
>>> *The glass is broken.*
>> **La ventana está <u>abierta</u>.**
>>> *The window is open.*
>> **Los empleados están <u>dispuestos</u>.**
>>> *The employees are willing.*

> Without **estar**
>> **La puerta <u>cerrada</u> es roja.**
>>> *The closed door is red.*
>> **El vaso <u>roto</u> era mi favorito.**
>>> *The broken glass was my favorite.*
>> **El perro <u>muerto</u> no ladra.**
>>> *The dead dog doesn't bark.*

There are several **irregular past participles**.

abrir / abierto	leer / leído
caer / caído	morir / muerto
creer / creído	oír / oído
cubrir / cubierto	poner / puesto
decir / dicho	reír / reído
descubrir / descubierto	resolver / resuelto
escribir / escrito	romper / roto
hacer / hecho	traer / traído
imprimir / impreso	ver / visto
ir / ido	volver / vuelto

The Tool Shed

10) FUTURE PERFECT

a) usually used for events that <u>will have taken place</u>.
   Ya <u>habrán llegado</u> cuando lleguemos nosotros.
   They will have arrived when we arrive.
   En un año <u>habré terminado</u> mis estudios.
   In a year, I will have finished my studies.

b) used to guess or <u>wonder about the future</u>.
   ¿<u>Habrán comido</u> todo?
   Will they have eaten everything?

*The **future perfect** is formed using the **future tense** of **haber**, and the **past participle**.

Future tense of **haber**:
habré, habrás, habrás, habremos, *habréis*, habrán

11) CONDITIONAL PERFECT

a) used to express <u>would have</u>.
   José <u>habría ido</u> si tuviera el dinero.
   Jose would have gone if he had the money.

b) used <u>to guess about the past</u>.
   Ella compró la casa. <u>Habría ganado</u> la lotería.
   She bought the house. She probably won the lottery.

*The **conditional perfect** is formed with the **conditional tense** of **haber**, and the **past participle**.

Conditional tense of **haber**:
habría, habrías, habría, habríamos, *habríais*, habrían

The **question words**, or **interrogatives**, (*who, what, where, when, why,* and *how*) are listed below, and then used in examples. In Spanish, all **interrogatives** carry a written accent when used in a question.

¿Quién?	*Who?*	**¿Cómo?**	*How?*
¿Quiénes?	*Who?* (plural)	**¿Por qué?**	*Why?*
¿Dónde?	*Where?*	**¿Cuál?**	*Which?*
¿Adónde?	*To where...?*	**¿Cuáles?**	*Which?* (plural)
¿Qué?	*What?*	**¿Cuánto/a/os/as?**	*How many?*

QUIEN, *who*

¿Quién es tu amigo?	*Who is your friend?*
¿Quién es el taxista?	*Who is the taxi driver?*
¿Quién eres?	*Who are you?*

QUIENES, *who* plural

¿Quiénes son los hermanos?	*Who are the brothers?*
¿Quiénes no comen carne?	*Who doesn't eat meat?*
¿Quiénes salen?	*Who is leaving?*

DONDE, *where*

¿Dónde está la playa?	*Where is the beach?*
¿Dónde está el aeropuerto?	*Where is the airport?*
¿Dónde consigues un taxi?	*Where do you get a taxi?*

ADONDE, *(to) where*, used with the verb **ir**

¿Adónde vas?	*Where are you going?*
¿Adónde va el autobús?	*Where does the bus go?*
¿Adónde vamos?	*Where are we going?*

QUE, *what*

¿Qué comen ellos?	*What are they eating? What do they eat?*
¿Qué hora es?	*What time is it?*
¿Qué tiempo hace?	*What is the weather like?*

The Tool Shed

COMO, *how, what*

¿Cómo estás?	*How are you?*
¿Cómo?	*What? (Pardon me?)*
¿Cómo te llamas?	*What is your name?*
	(How do you call yourself?)
¿Cómo es la casa?	*What is the house like?*

POR QUE, *why*

¿Por qué hay tráfico?	*Why is there traffic?*
¿Por qué no salimos?	*Why don't we leave?*
¿Por qué no?	*Why not?*

CUAL, *which*

¿Cuál es la mejor escuela?	*Which is the best school?*
¿Cuál es mi vuelo?	*Which is my flight?*
¿Cuál prefieres?	*Which do you prefer?*

CUALES, *which* plural

¿Cuáles son los mejores?	*Which are the best?*
¿Cuáles te gustan?	*Which do you like?*
¿Cuáles frutas comes?	*Which fruits do you eat?*

CUANTO (a/os/as), *how many, how much*

¿Cuántas hermanas tienes?	*How many sisters do you have?*
¿Cuánto dinero tienes?	*How much money do you have?*
¿Cuántos cursos tomas?	*How many classes are you taking?*

The Tool Shed

KEY IRREGULAR VERBS

infinitive, participles	present	Imperfect	preterite	future
DECIR *say or tell* diciendo dicho	digo dices dice decimos *decís* dicen	decía decías decía decíamos *deciais* decían	dije dijiste dijo dijimos *dijisteis* dijeron	diré dirás dirá diremos *diréis* dirán
ESTAR *to be* estando estado	estoy estás está estamos *estais* están	estaba estabas estaba estábamos *estabais* estaban	estuve estuviste estuvo estuvimos *estuvisteis* estuvieron	estaré estarás estará estaremos *estaréis* estarán
HACER *to do or make* haciendo hecho	hago haces hace hacemos *hacéis* hacen	hacía hacías hacía hacíamos *hacíais* hacían	hice hiciste hizo hicimos *hicisteis* hicieron	haré harás hará haremos *haréis* harán
IR *to go* yendo ido	voy vas va vamos *vais* van	iba ibas iba íbamos *ibais* iban	fui fuiste fue fuimos *fuisteis* fueron	iré irás irá iremos *iréis* irán
SER *to be* siendo sido	soy eres es somos *sois* son	era eras era éramos *erais* eran	fui fuiste fue fuimos *fusteis* fueron	seré serás será seremos *seréis* serán
TENER *to have* teniendo tenido	tengo tienes tiene tenemos *tenéis* tienen	tenía tenías tenía teníamos *teníais* tenían	tuve tuviste tuvo tuvimos *tuvisteis* tuvieron	tendré tendrás tendrá tendremos *tendréis* tendrán

The Tool Shed

KEY IRREGULAR VERBS

infinitive, participles	conditional	present subjunctive	imperfect subjunctive	commands
DECIR	diría	diga	dijera	TU
say or tell	dirías	digas	dijeras	di
	diría	diga	dijera	no digas
diciendo	diríamos	digamos	dijéramos	USTED
dicho	*diríais*	*digais*	*dijerais*	diga
	dirían	digan	dijeran	no diga
ESTAR	estaría	esté	estuviera	TU
to be	estarías	estés	estuvieras	está
	estaría	esté	estviera	no estés
estando	estaríamos	estemos	estuviéramos	USTED
estado	*estaríais*	*estéis*	*estuvierais*	esté
	estarían	estén	estuvieran	no esté
HACER	haría	haga	hiciera	TU
to do or make	harías	hagas	hicieras	haz
	haría	haga	hiciera	no hagas
haciendo	haríamos	hagamos	hiciéramos	USTED
hecho	*haríais*	*hagáis*	*hicierais*	haga
	harían	hagan	hicieran	no haga
IR	iría	vaya	fuera	TU
to go	irías	vayas	fueras	ve
	iría	vaya	fuera	no vayas
yendo	iríamos	vayamos	fuéramos	USTED
ido	*iríais*	*vayáis*	*fuerais*	vaya
	irían	vayan	fueran	no vaya
SER	sería	sea	fuera	TU
to be	serías	seas	fueras	sé
	sería	sea	fuera	no seas
siendo	seríamos	seamos	fuéramos	USTED
sido	*seríais*	*seáis*	*fuerais*	sea
	serían	sean	fueran	no sea
TENER	tendría	tenga	tuviera	TU
to have	tendrías	tengas	tuvieras	ten
	tendría	tenga	tuviera	no tengas
teniendo	tendríamos	tengamos	tuviéramos	USTED
tenido	*tendríais*	*tengáis*	*tuvierais*	tenga
	tendrán	tengan	tuvieran	no tenga

The Tool Shed

COMMON IRREGULAR VERBS IN EACH TENSE

PRESENT TENSE

ESTAR, *to be*	HABER, *to have (aux verb)*	IR, *to go*	OIR, *to hear*	SER, *to be*
estoy	he	voy	oigo	soy
estás	has	vas	oyes	eres
está	ha	va	oye	es
estamos	hemos	vamos	oímos	somos
estáis	*habéis*	*vais*	*oís*	*sois*
están	han	van	oyen	son

PRESENT TENSE, irregular **yo** forms

caber – quepo	dar – doy	saber – sé	valer – valgo
caer – caigo	decir – digo	salir – salgo	venir – vengo
conducir – conduzco	hacer – hago	tener – tengo	ver – veo
conocer – conozco	poner – pongo	traer – traigo	

PRETERITE VERBS

DAR	LEER	PODER	PONER	QUERER
di	leí	pude	puse	quise
diste	leíste	pudiste	pusiste	quisiste
dio	leyó	pudo	puso	quiso
dimos	leímos	pudimos	pusimos	quisimos
disteis	*leísteis*	*pudisteis*	*pusisteis*	*queréis*
dieron	leyeron	pudieron	pusieron	quisieron
SABER	TRAER	VENIR	VER	
supe	traje	vine	vi	
supiste	trajiste	viniste	viste	
supo	trajo	vino	vio	
supimos	trajimos	vinimos	vimos	
sabéis	*traéis*	*vinisteis*	*visteis*	
supieron	trajeron	vinieron	vieron	

FUTURE AND CONDITIONAL IRREGULAR STEMS

caber – cabr	hacer – har	querer – querr	tener – tendr
decir – dir	poder – podr	saber – sabr	valer – valdr
haber – habr	poner – pondr	salir – saldr	venir – vendr

The Tool Shed

PRONUNCIATION

🔑 Spanish is pronounced as it is written. For the most part, each letter makes the same sound all of the time. Unlike in English, there are very few irregularities in pronunciation or in spelling.

letter	name	English sound	Spanish Example	
a	a	**a**wesome	**A**na	(AH-na)
b	be, be grande	**b**ay	**b**ata	(BAH-tuh)
c	ce	**s**ay	**c**ena	(SAY-na)
d	de	**d**ay	**d**ía	(DEE-ah)
e	e	h**ey**	**efe**cto	(eh-FEC-toe)
f	efe	**f**ield	**f**ino	(FEE-no)
g	ge	**h**ay	**g**ente	(HEN-te)
h	hache	**silent letter!**	**h**ijo	(EE-hoe)
i	i	b**ee**tle	t**i**po	(TEE-poe)
j	jota	**h**ay	**j**abón	(ha-BONE)
k	ca	hac**k**	**k**ilo	(KI-loe)
l	ele	**l**oad	**l**odo	(LOW-tho)
m	eme	**m**e	**m**odo	(MOE-tho)
n	ene	**n**ote	**n**ativo	(naw-TEE-voe)
ñ	eñe	ca**ny**on	ni**ñ**o	(NEE-nyo)
o	o	b**o**at	b**o**ca	(BOE-ca)
p	pe	**p**ine	**p**ino	(PEE-no)
q	cu	dis**k**	**q**uesadilla	(kay-sa-DEE-ya)
r	ere	la**dd**er	pe**r**o	(PEDD-oh)
s	ese	li**s**t	e**s**pero	(es-PEDD-oh)
t	te	**t**oad	tor**t**a	(TOR-tah)
u	u	d**u**et	**u**va	(EW-bah)
v	ve, ve chica	**b**ay	**v**aso	(BAH-soe)
w	doble u	to**w**	**w**aleta	(wah-LET-uh)
x	equis	te**x**ture	e**x**tra	(EX-tra)
y	I griega	**y**odel	a**y**er	(AH-yer)
z	zeta	**s**ea	**z**apato	(sa-PA-toe)

The Tool Shed

ACCENTS, STRESSING SYLLABLE, AND COMBINATIONS

ACCENTS AND STRESS

Just as in English, some syllables are stressed more than others. See the following rules:

1) When a word ends in a vowel, n, or s, the stress is usually on the next-to-last syllable.

libro (LI-broe)   **ca**sa (KA-suh)   mo**ne**da (moe-NAY-tha)

2) When a word ends in a consonant, but is not n or s, the stress usually falls on the last syllable.

pin**cel** (peen-CEL)   co**mer** (koe-MER)   do**blez** (doe-BLESS)

3) When a word does not follow the above rules, there is a written accent.

lápiz (LA-pees)   rin**cón** (reen-CONE)   bo**lí**grafo (boe-LEE-grah-foe)

COMBINATIONS AND ANOMALIES

ll   When an "l" comes next to another "l," the result is a "y" sound, as in "your" in English. The double "l" appears in the following words.

ga**ll**o (GUY-yo)   **ll**ano (YA-noe)

rr   The double "r" has the sound of a rolled "r." It might be difficult to make this sound. The double "r" is produced by repeatedly flapping the tongue against the roof and front of the mouth. When the single "r" comes at the beginning of a word, like in Roberto, it has the double "r" sound (the rolled "r").

rojo (ROE-hoe)   tie**rr**a (tee-AIR-uh)

r   The single letter "r" is not quite as strong as the "r" in English (except as mentioned above). The "r" can have a sound similar to the English letter "d" as in "ladder," or the English "t" as in "better" or "butter."

pa**r**a (PA-da)   dine**r**o (dee-NET-oe)

d   The letter "d" is pronounced similarly to the English "d" when it occurs at the beginning of a word, or after a consonant.

don**d**e (DOEN-day)   **d**ías (DEE-us)

The Tool Shed

When the Spanish "d" occurs after a vowel, the "d" is softened and has more of a "th" sound as in the word "brother."

criada (cree-AH-tha)   nada (NAH-tha)

s The Spanish letter "s" usually makes a sound similar to the English "s" as in "sit."

espero (es-PEDD-oh)   días (DEE-us)

When the Spanish "s" comes before "b," "d," "g," "l," "m," and "n" in speech it makes the English "z" sound.

desde (DEZ-day)   asno (AHZ-noe)

t In Spanish, the letter "t" is pronounced similar to the "t" in English, though without aspiration. Aspiration is the air that comes out of the mouth in a little explosion, as in the English word "tie." In Spanish, air does not forcefully come out of the mouth.

todo (TOE-tho)   cinta (SEEN-ta)

c When the Spanish letter "c" comes before "a," "o," "u," or a consonant, it makes the "k" sound as in "can."

caña (KAH-nya)   cola (KOH-la)

When the letter "c" comes before "e" or "i", the Spanish letter "c" is pronounced like "s" as in the English "sound."

centro (SEN-troe)   cine (SEE-nay)

j The letter "j" is not similar to the English "j." In Spanish, the "j" is pronounced similarly to the English "h" as in "hen."

viaje (bee-AH-hay)   rojo (ROE-hoe)

g The "g" has two distinct pronunciations. Before the vowels "e" and "i" the Spanish "g" is pronounced like the English "h" as in "hen."

agente (ah-HEN-tay)   ágil (AH-heel)

When the "g" comes after "n," it has a sound like the English "goat."

venganza (ben-GAHN-suh)   mango (MAHN-go)

When the "g" comes in the combination "gue" or "gui," the "u" is silent.

guía (GEE-uh)   guerra (GAIR-uh)

ñ The "ñ" is produced nasally, and is similar to the English "ny" sound as in "canyon" or the "ni" as in "minion."

mañana (ma-NYA-na)   español (es-pah-NYOL)

The Tool Shed

v The letter "v" is pronounced similarly to the English "b," although it is not aspirated (a puff of air does not leave your mouth when it is pronounced as in the English "b," as in "boy").

veinte (BANE-tay)   in**v**ierno (in-be-AIR-no)

h The Spanish letter "h" is silent. It is the only letter that is silent all the time.

hijo (EE-hoe)   **h**ormiga (or-MEE-guh)

x The Spanish "x" has three sounds. After the "e," and "i," the "x" has a sound similar to the English sound in "extra."

e**x**ótico (ex-OH-ti-coe)   I**x**tapa (ixs-TAH-puh)

When the "x" appears in most place names and some proper names, it has the sound of the Spanish "j" (which is similar to the English "h").

Mé**x**ico (MEH-he-coe)   **X**avier (ha-bee-AIR)   Te**x**as (TEH-hoss)

The Spanish "x" will also occasionally have the English "sh" sound, as in "shut." This sound is rarely found, though usually associated with proper names.

Xu**x**a (SHOE-sha)   **X**imena (she-MEN-ah)

z In Latin America, the Spanish letter "z" almost never makes the English "z" sound as in "zoo." Rather, the Spanish letter "z" usually makes the English "s."

zapato (sah-PAW-toe)   die**z** (dee-ESS)

qu The combination "qu" is pronounced like "c" in the English "can." Like the Spanish "t" sound, the "qu" is not aspirated.

que (KAY)   **qu**iero (key-AIR-oh)

DIPHTHONGS

When two vowels occur next to each other in a syllable they sometimes produce a single sound. This is called a **diphthong**. Specifically, when a hard vowel (**a**, **e**, or **o**) is next to a soft vowel (**i** or **u**), or when two soft vowels are next to each other, the result is a **diphthong**.

v**ei**nte (VANE-tay)   b**ue**no (BWEH-no)

When **i** or **u** comes after a vowel and has a written accent mark, the **diphthong** is annulled and the combination is pronounced as two syllables.

p**aí**s (pah-EES)   **oí**r (oh-EER)

The Tool Shed

MAKING WORDS MATCH

NOUNS, GENDER & NUMBER

In Spanish, <u>all nouns are either masculine or feminine</u>. <u>This is known as **gender**</u>. This does not mean that nouns have masculine or feminine characteristics, **gender** is just a way of organizing words. <u>If a noun ends in **o,** it is usually masculine</u>. <u>If a noun ends in **a,** it is usually feminine</u>. Most nouns that end in **ion, dad, tad, tud** and **umbre** are also feminine. Nouns are also either <u>singular or plural: this is known as **number**</u>. If a noun ends in **a** or **o,** it can be made plural by adding **s**. If a noun ends in a consonant, add **es** to make it plural.

MASCULINE NOUNS AND ARTICLES		FEMININE NOUNS AND ARTICLES	
el perro	*the dog*	**la tienda**	*the store*
los perros	*the dogs*	**las tiendas**	*the stores*
el zapato	*the shoe*	**la puerta**	*the door*
los zapatos	*the shoes*	**las puertas**	*the doors*
el reloj	*the watch*	**la libertad**	*the liberty*
los relojes	*the watches*	**las libertades**	*the liberties*

NOUNS THAT REFER TO PEOPLE

<u>Nouns that refer to males are masculine, and nouns that refer to females are feminine</u>. Some nouns that refer to people indicate **gender** by changing the last vowel (**médico/médica**). Some nouns that refer to people only have one form, like **dentista**; gender is distinguished by the article (**el, la, los, las**). When a masculine noun ends in a consonant, **a** is added to the consonant to indicate a female (**conductor/conductora**). Below are some examples of nouns that refer to people.

MASCULINE NOUNS		FEMININE NOUNS	
el mesero	*the waiter*	**la mesera**	*the waitress*
el hombre	*the man*	**la mujer**	*the woman*
el profesor	*the (male) teacher*	**la profesora**	*the (female) teacher*
el conductor	*the (male) driver*	**la conductora**	*the (female) driver*
el dentista	*the (male) dentist*	**la dentista**	*the (female) dentist*

The Tool Shed

ARTICLES

Articles change for **gender** and **number**, and must match the noun. This means that if a noun is feminine, for example, the **article** must be feminine. There are **definite articles** (*the*) and **indefinite articles** (*a, some*).

DEFINITE ARTICLES, el, la, los, las

	MASCULINE		FEMININE	
singular	**el** perro	*the dog*	**la** tienda	*the store*
plural	**los** perros	*the* dogs	**las** tiendas	*the stores*

INDEFINITE ARTICLES, un, una, unos, unas

	MASCULINE		FEMININE	
singular	**un** perro	*a dog*	**una** tienda	*a store*
plural	**unos** perros	*some dogs*	**unas** tiendas	*some stores*

ADJECTIVES

Adjectives (words that describe nouns) must also match the noun for both **gender** and **number**. For example, if the noun is singular and masculine, the **adjective** must also be singular and masculine. In the sentences below, notice how the article and **adjective** match the noun for **gender** and **number**. Usually, **adjectives** come after the noun they are describing.

el **libro** nuevo	*the new book*
los **libros** nuevos	*the new books*
un **perro** loco	*a crazy dog*
unos **perros** locos	*some crazy dogs*
la **chica** alta	*the tall girl*
las **chicas** altas	*the tall girls*
una **tienda** roja	*a red store*
unas **tiendas** rojas	*some red stores*

If an **adjective** does not end in **o** or **a**, it will only change for number, not gender (**grande/grandes**, **amable/amables**).

The Tool Shed

GENDER EXCEPTIONS

There are some nouns that do not follow the rule for **gender**. Some of the more common exceptions follow.

MASCULINE WORDS THAT END IN "A"   **FEMININE WORDS THAT END IN "O"**

el agua	*the water*	**la disco**	*the discotheque*
el clima	*the climate*	*(short for* **discoteca***)*	
el cometa	*the comet*	**la foto**	*the photo*
el drama	*the drama*	*(short for* **fotografía***)*	
el día	*the day*	**la mano**	*the hand*
el fantasma	*the ghost*	**la moto**	*the motorcycle*
el idioma	*the language*	*(short for* **motocicleta***)*	
el mapa	*the map*		
el planeta	*the planet*		
el poema	*the poem*		
el problema	*the problem*		
el sistema	*the system*		
el sofá	*the sofa*		
el yoga	*the yoga*		

The Tool Shed

 EXERCISES: MAKING WORDS MATCH: GENDER AND NUMBER

Use a **definite article: el, la, los, las.**   Use an **indefinite article: un, una, unos, unas.**

1. ____ **playa**	*the* beach	
2. ____ **casa**	*the* house	
3. ____ **vasos**	*the* glasses	
4. ____ **patio**	*the* patio	
5. ____ **sillas**	*the* chairs	
6. ____ **plato**	*the* plates	
7. ____ **cara**	*the* face	
8. ____ **mesas**	*the* tables	
9. ____ **jarra**	*the* jar	
10. ____ **dinero**	*the* money	
11. ____ **cuchillo**	*the* knife	
12. ____ **palos**	*the* sticks	
13. ____ **latas**	*the* cans	
14. ____ **cera**	*the* wax	
15. ____ **arena**	*the* sand	

1. ____ **lobos**	*some* wolves
2. ____ **pato**	*a* duck
3. ____ **planta**	*a* plant
4. ____ **tazas**	*some* cups
5. ____ **vela**	*a* candle
6. ____ **plumas**	*some* pens
7. ____ **página**	*a* page
8. ____ **conejos**	*some* rabbits
9. ____ **cerveza**	*a* beer
10. ____ **mangos**	*some* mangos
11. ____ **papas**	*some* potatos
12. ____ **pera**	*a* pair
13. ____ **ratas**	*some* rats
14. ____ **puerta**	*a* door
15. ____ **primos**	*some* cousins

Change the **adjective** to match the **noun.**

1. niña _____	(alto)	11. solicitud _____	(largo)
2. amigos _____	(íntimo)	12. niños _____	(bajo)
3. mango _____	(amarillo)	13. carpeta _____	(morado)
4. padres _____	(generoso)	14. sacos _____	(suave)
5. casa _____	(antiguo)	15. pasto _____	(bonito)
6. caminos _____	(recto)	16. libros _____	(grande)
7. rancho _____	(extenso)	17. islas _____	(encantado)
8. mamás _____	(amable)	18. barco _____	(pequeño)
9. silla _____	(blanco)	19. horno _____	(apagado)
10. taza _____	(viejo)	20. camisa _____	(roto)

The Tool Shed

Put a **definite or indefinite article** in the first blank. In the second blank, put a form of the **adjective** in parenthesis.

Example: **<u>unos</u> barcos <u>nuevos</u> (nuevo)**   <u>some</u> new boats

1. _____ **botella** _____ **(roto)**	<u>a</u> broken bottle
2. _____ **cena** _____ **(bueno)**	<u>the</u> good dinner
3. _____ **caballos** _____ **(hermoso)**	<u>some</u> lovely horses
4. _____ **burritos** _____ **(sabroso)**	<u>the</u> tasty burritos
5. _____ **llantas** _____ **(negro)**	<u>the</u> black tires
6. _____ **vidrio** _____ **(limpio)**	<u>the</u> clean glass
7. _____ **lámpara** _____ **(rojo)**	<u>a</u> red lamp
8. _____ **pollos** _____ **(asado)**	<u>some</u> grilled chickens
9. _____ **niño** _____ **(travieso)**	<u>the</u> mischievous boy
10. _____ **carros** _____ **(caro)**	<u>some</u> expensive cars

ANSWERS TO EXERCISES: MAKING WORDS MATCH: GENDER AND NUMBER

Use a **definite article: el, la, los, las.**

1. la
2. la
3. los
4. el
5. las
6. el
7. la
8. las
9. la
10. el
11. el
12. los
13. las
14. la
15. la

Use an **indefinite article: un, una, unos, unas.**

1. unos
2. un
3. una
4. unas
5. una
6. unas
7. una
8. unos
9. una
10. unos
11. unas
12. una
13. unas
14. una
15. unos

The Tool Shed

Change the **adjective** to match the **noun**.

1. alta
2. íntimos
3. amarillo
4. generosos
5. antigua
6. rectos
7. extenso
8. amables
9. blanca
10. vieja
11. larga
12. bajos
13. morada
14. suaves
15. bonito
16. grandes
17. encantadas
18. pequeño
19. apagado
20. rota

Put a **definite or indefinite article** in the first blank. In the second blank, put a form of the **adjective** in parenthesis.

1. una, rota
2. la, buena
3. unos, hermosos
4. los, sabrosos
5. las, negras
6. el, limpio
7. una, roja
8. unos, asados
9. el, travieso
10. unos, caros

The Tool Shed

POSSESSION

There are three ways to communicate possession or ownership.

The first option is to put the article and noun first, followed by "de" (of), and then state the owner. For example, **el libro de Eduardo** (*the book of Eduardo*), or **el carro de Juan** (*the car of Juan*). The apostrophe "s" (ie. Steve's job) does not exist in Spanish.

la corbata de Juan	*Juan's tie (The tie of Juan)*
la casa de Jorge	*Jorge's house (The house of Jorge)*
el perro de Julia	*Julia's dog (The dog of Julia)*

The second option is to use a possessive adjective. These adjectives are placed before a noun. Notice that only **nuestro** changes for gender and number. The other forms (*my, your, his*, etc.), only change for number. Also, notice that **su** and **sus** are used for *her, his, your* (formal), and the plural *their*, and *your* (plural). See below.

my	mi	mi casa	my house
	mis	mis casas	my houses
your	tu	tu mesa	your table
	tus	tus mesas	your tables
his/hers/	su	su amigo	his/her/your (formal) friend
your (formal)	sus	sus amigos	his/her/your (formal) friends
our	nuestro	nuestro perro	our dog
	nuestra	nuestra casa	our house
	nuestros	nuestros perros	our dogs
	nuestras	nuestras casas	our houses
their/	su	su libro	their book, your (plural) book
your (plural)	sus	sus libros	their book, your (plural) books

The third option is to use a possessive pronoun. These change for gender and number and are placed after the article and noun.

my	mío/a	el carro mío	My car
	míos/as	los carros míos	My cars
your	tuyo/a	el libro tuyo	Your book
	tuyos/as	los libros tuyos	Your books
his/hers/	suyo	el amigo suyo	his/hers/your (formal) friend
your (formal)	suya	la caja suya	his/her/your (formal) box
	suyos	los amigos suyos	his/hers/your (formal) friends
	suyas	las cajas suyas	his/her/your (formal) boxes
our	nuestro	el gato nuestro	our cat
	nuestra	la casa nuestra	our house
	nuestros	los gatos nuestros	our cats
	nuestras	las casas nuestras	our houses
their/	suyo	el libro suyo	their book, your (plural) book
your (plural)	suya	la mesa suya	their table, your (plural) table
	suyos	los libros suyos	their book, your (plural) books
	suyas	las mesas suyas	their tables, your (plural) tables

The Tool Shed

 EXERCISES: POSESSION

Showing Possession. Follow the models in each section.

las casas de Juan	**Juan's houses (the houses of Juan)**

1. _____ Lalo's car (the car of Lalo)
2. _____ Julio's book (the book of Julio)
3. _____ the girls' cousin (the cousin of the girls)
4. _____ Ana's project (the project of Ana)
5. _____ Lola's garden (the garden of Lola)
6. _____ Chato's chickens (the chickens of Chato)
7. _____ Lao's class (the class of Lao)
8. _____ the friends' house (the house of the friends)
9. _____ Sara's business (the business of Sara)
10._____ Nina's job (the job of Nina)

mis casas	*my houses*

11. _____ *your dog*
12. _____ *her money*
13. _____ *their book*
14. _____ *his book*
15. _____ *our mangos*
16. _____ *my cat*
17. _____ *her pencils*
18. _____ *your apartments*
19. _____ *our door*
20. _____ *our folders*

las casas mías	*my houses*

21. _____ *her lunch*
22. _____ *his jobs*
23. _____ *our beaches*
24. _____ *their fruit*
25. _____ *your* (plural) *chairs*
26. _____ *my students*
27. _____ *my city*
28. _____ *our cars*
29. _____ *their tables*
30. _____ *your* (plural) *food*

ANSWERS TO EXERCISES: POSESSION

Showing Possession. Follow the models in each section.

las casas de Juan
1. el coche de Lalo
2. el libro de Julio
3. el primo de las chicas
4. el proyecto de Ana
5. el jardín de Lola
6. los pollos de Chato
7. la clase de Lao
8. la casa de los amigos
9. el negocio de Sara
10. el trabajo de Nina

mis casas
11. tu perro
12. su dinero
13. su libro
14. su libro
15. nuestros mangos
16. mi gato
17. sus lápices
18. tus apartamentos
19. nuestra puerta
20. nuestras carpetas

las casas mías
21. el almuerzo suyo
22. los trabajos suyos
23. las playas nuestras
24. la fruta suya
25. las sillas suyas
26. los estudiantes míos
27. la ciudad mía
28. los coches nuestros
29. las mesas suyas
30. la comida suya

The Tool Shed

TELLING TIME

There are specific patterns to follow when talking about the time in Spanish. Below are examples of how to ask the time, ask what time an event begins, and how to answer these questions.

ASKING THE TIME

To ask the time, the question is:

¿Qué hora es? *What time is it?*

TELLING THE TIME

There are two ways to tell the time.

1) **Between the hours of 2:00 and 12:00**, start by saying **Son las** and then tell the time:

Son las _____.	*It is _____.*
Son las cinco.	*It is 5:00.*
Son las ocho y quince.	*It is 8:15.*
Son las dos.	*It is 2:00.*
Son las dos y cinco.	*It is 2:05.*
Son las dos y doce.	*It is 2:12.*
Son las dos y veinticinco.	*It is 2:25.*

2) During the **one o'clock hour (1:00…)**, start by saying **Es la** and then tell the time:

Es la _____.	*It is _____.*
Es la una y dos.	*It is 1:02.*
Es la una y media.	*It is 1:30.*
Es la una.	*It is 1:00.*
Es la una y diez.	*It is 1:10.*
Es la una y catorce.	*It is 1:14.*
Es la una y veintidós.	*It is 1:22.*

TELLING TIME PAST 30 MINUTES INTO THE HOUR

When you are telling time, and it is more than half past the hour, it is very common to go to the next hour and subtract the minutes. For example, if the time is 2:50, it is often stated as *3:00 o'clock minus 10*. The speaker goes to the next hour, and subtracts the minutes remaining.

5:45	**Son las seis, menos quince (or cuarto).**
10:55	**Son las once, menos cinco.**
11:40	**Son las doce, menos veinte.**
12:35	**Es la una menos veinticinco.**
1:57	**Son las dos menos tres.**

ASKING WHAT TIME AN EVENT BEGINS

When you are asking **what time an event begins,** the question begins with **A**… and translates to *At…*

¿A qué hora es la clase?	*(At) what time is the class?*
¿A qué hora es el almuerzo?	*(At) what time is lunch?*
¿A qué hora es el vuelo?	*(At) what time is the flight?*

TELLING WHAT TIME AN EVENT BEGINS

El desfile es a las doce y cinco.	*The parade is at 12:05.*
La boda es a las tres.	*The wedding is at 3:00.*
El almuerzo es a las diez y media.	*The lunch is at 10:30.*

TELLING WHAT TIME AN EVENT TAKES PLACE, WITHOUT MENTIONING THE EVENT.

Es a las doce y cinco.	*It's at 12:05.*
Es a las tres.	*It's at 3:00.*
Es a las diez y media.	*It's at 10:30.*

The Tool Shed

WORDS FREQUENTLY ASSOCIATED WITH TELLING TIME

There are a few words and phrases associated with talking about the time:

cuarto	**Es la una y <u>cuarto</u>**. *(fifteen or quarter)*
media	**Son las seis y <u>media</u>**. *(thirty or half-past)*
la medianoche	**Es la <u>medianoche</u>**. *(midnight)*
el mediodía	**Es el <u>mediodía</u>**. *(noon)*
en punto	**Son las dos en <u>punto</u>**. *(exactly)*
de la mañana	**Son las dos de la <u>mañana</u>**. *(in the morning)*
de la tarde	**Son las cuatro de la <u>tarde</u>**. *(in the afternoon)*
de la noche	**Son las diez de la <u>noche</u>**. *(in the evening)*

The Tool Shed

ASKING & TELLING HOW LONG SOMETHING HAS BEEN HAPPENING

To ASK how long an activity has been going on, use a verb in the present tense, and the following formula:

¿Cuánto tiempo hace que + verb? (the verb must be in the present tense)

¿Cuánto tiempo hace que nadas?   *How long have you been swimming?*

To TELL how long an activity has been going on, use the formula below:

Hace + time period + que + verb (the verb must be in the present tense)

Hace una hora que nado.   *I have been swimming for one hour.*

Below are questions and answers, asking and telling how long an activity has been going on.

1) ¿Cuánto tiempo hace que cocinas?
How long have you been cooking?

Hace un año que cocino.
I have been cooking for one year.

2) ¿Cuánto tiempo hace que viajas?
How long have you been traveling?

Hace dos semanas que viajo.
I've been traveling for two weeks.

3) ¿Cuánto tiempo hace que estudias?
How long have you been studying?

Hace tres meses que estudio.
I've been studying for three months.

4) ¿Cuánto tiempo hace que no tomas?
How long have you not been drinking?

Hace cinco años que no tomo.
I haven't been drinking for five years.

5) ¿Cuánto tiempo hace que esperas aquí?
How long have you been waiting here?

Hace veinte minutos que espero aquí.
I've been waiting here for twenty minutes.

The Tool Shed

To ASK or TELL how long ago something took place, use the same construction as above, but change the verb to the **preterite** (past) tense. See the questions and answers below.

1) ¿Cuánto tiempo hace que hablaste con Jaime?
How long has it been since you spoke with Jaime?

Hace diez minutos que hablé con Jaime.
I spoke with Jaime ten minutes ago.

2) ¿Cuánto tiempo hace que comiste?
How long has it been since you ate?

Hace un día que comí.
It has been one day since I ate.

3) ¿Cuánto tiempo hace que pagaste?
How long ago did you pay?

Hace una semana que pagué.
It has been one week since I paid.

4) ¿Cuánto tiempo hace que lo compraste?
How long ago did you buy it?

Hace un mes que lo compré?
I bought it one month ago.

5) ¿Cuánto tiempo hace que esperaste?
How long has it been since you waited?

Hace unos meses que esperé.
It's been a few months since I waited.

The Tool Shed

 EXERCISES: TELLING TIME

TIME EXERCISES

Tell the time in Spanish. If the hour is past 30 minutes, go to the next hour and subtract the minutes.

1. 2:30 _____
2. 1:10 _____
3. 6:50 _____
4. 4:20 _____
5. 12:45 _____
6. 9:01 _____
7. 11:30 _____
8. 12:00 _____
9. 7:15 _____
10. 11:23 _____

Ask what time the following events take place.

11. _____   **La boda es a las once y veinticuatro.**
The wedding is at 11:24.

12. _____   **La clase es a la una en punto.**
The class is at one sharp.

13. _____   **El programa es a las siete.**
The program is at seven.

Answer the following questions.

14. **¿A qué hora es la misa?**   _____
The mass is at 12:00.

15. **¿A qué hora es el partido?**   _____
The game is at 1:10.

16. **¿A qué hora es la charla?**   _____
The chat is at 6:05.

The Tool Shed

Answer in the present or past according to the cues. Use **hace que** in your answers.

17. **¿Cuánto tiempo hace que saliste del país?** _____

    How long ago since you left the country?   *It has been 6 months since I left the country.*

18. **¿Cuánto tiempo hace que compras ropa?** _____

    How long have you been buying clothes?   *I have been buying clothes for 2 hours.*

19. **¿Cuánto tiempo hace que comiste el pez?** _____

    How long ago since you ate the fish?   *I ate the fish 10 minutes ago.*

ANSWERS TO EXERCISES: TELLING TIME

Tell the time in Spanish. If the hour is past 30 minutes, go to the next hour and subtract the minutes.

1. Son las dos y media (treinta).
2. Es la una y diez.
3. Son las siete menos diez.
4. Son las cuatro y veinte.
5. Es la una menos cuarto (quince).
6. Son las nueve y uno.
7. Son las once y media.
8. Son las doce.
9. Son las siete y cuarto (quince).
10. Son las once y veintitrés.

Ask what time the following events take place.
11. ¿A qué hora es la boda?
12. ¿A qué hora es la clase?
13. ¿A qué hora es el programa?

Answer the following questions.
14. La misa es a las doce.
15. El partido es a la una y diez.
16. La charla es a las seis y cinco.

Answer in the present or past according to the cues. Use hace que in your answers.
17. Hace seis meses que salí del país.
18. Hace dos horas que compro ropa.
19. Hace diez minutos que comí el pescado.

CHAPTER 20

The Tool Shed

DEMONSTRATIVE ADJECTIVES & PRONOUNS

THIS & THESE, THAT & THOSE

We use **demonstrative adjectives** to describe where something is located. They change for gender and number. Which adjective is used depends on how far the speaker is from the object.

	este/estos	*this*
close	**esta/estas**	*these*

	ese/esos	*that*
medium	**esa/esas**	*those*

	aquel/aquellos	*that (over there)*
far	**aquella/aquellas**	*those (over there)*

Speaker

Este carro es grande.	*This car is big.*
Estos carros son grandes.	*These cars are big.*
Esa casa es azul.	*That house is blue.*
Esas casas son azules.	*Those houses are blue.*
Aquel puente es largo.	*That bridge (over there) is long.*
Aquellos puentes son largos.	*Those bridges (over there) are long.*

When **este**, **ese**, and **aquel** are used without the noun being referenced, they are **demonstrative pronouns**, and they usually carry an accent. Although they often have an accent, it is no longer required.

¿Viste su carro?	**Sí, ése es un modelo costoso.**
Did you see his car?	*Yes, that is a costly model.*
Mira los caballos.	**Aquéllos son hermosos.**
Look at those horses.	*Those (over there) are lovely.*

There are **neuter demonstrative pronouns** as well (**esto, eso, aquello**). These pronouns are used when the object, idea, concept, or circumstance has not been identified.

Esto no me agrada.	*This doesn't please me.*
¿Qué es eso?	*What is that?*
Aquello es otro asunto.	*That is another matter.*

The Tool Shed

CHAPTER 21

COMPARISONS

COMPARING ADJECTIVES AND ADVERBS

Equal

tan + adj/adv + **como**

Juana habla tan bien como Lola.
Juana speaks as well as Lola.

Unequal

mas/menos + adj/adv + **que**

Ed es menos flojo que Yolo.
Ed is less lazy than Yolo.
(Ed is not as lazy as Yolo.)

COMPARING NOUNS

Equal

tanto/a/os/as + noun + **como**

Hay tantos gatos como perros.
There are as many cats as dogs.

Unequal

más/menos + noun + **que**

Hay menos carros que camionetas.
There are less cars than trucks.

The preposition **de** is used when the comparison is followed by a number.

más/menos + **de** + number + noun

Yo tengo más de veinte gatos.
I have more than twenty cats.

COMPARING VERBS

Equal

verb + **tanto como**

Hablo tanto como Ramona.
I speak as much as Ramona.

Unequal

verb + **más/menos** + **que**

Corro menos que John.
I run less than John.

THE SUPERLATIVE (THE LEAST, THE BEST, THE GREATEST)

definite article + **más/menos** + adjective

Juan es el más listo de la clase.
Juan is the smartest of the class.

Ellas son las menos altas del grupo.
They are the least tall of the group.

CHAPTER 22

The Tool Shed

CONTRACTIONS

There are two contractions (combining two words into one) in Spanish. Unlike English, contractions must be used when circumstances dictate.

The first contraction is **al** *(to the)*. When **a** comes next to the article **el**, the words merge and become **al**.

Vamos al (a+el) hotel.	*Let's go to the hotel.*
Ellos van al (a+el) mercado.	*They go to the market.*
Juana va al (a+el) rastro.	*Juana goes to the flea market.*

The second contraction is **del** *(of the)*. When **de** comes next to the article **el**, the result is **del**. This contraction is used with possession.

La casa del (de+el) hombre.	*The man's house. (The house of the man.)*
El perro del (de+el) niño.	*The boy's dog. (The dog of the boy.)*
El libro del (de+el) estudiante.	*The student's book. (The book of the student.)*

The Tool Shed

CHAPTER 23

STEM-CHANGING VERBS

PRESENT TENSE Stem-changing verbs change in the stem in all forms except **nosotros** and *vosotros*. The change always occurs with a vowel: one vowel will be changed to two, or one vowel will be replaced by another. Below are examples from each stem-changing group, and similar verbs. There are several different kinds of stem-changes.

E to IE stem-changing verbs

PENSAR: pienso, piensas, piensa, pensamos, *penséis*, **piensan**

apretar	divertirse	helar	querer
cerrar	empezar	nevar	recomendar
comenzar	encender	perder	sentarse
despertarse	entender	quebrar	sentirse

O to UE stem-changing verbs

DORMIR: duermo, duermes, duerme, dormimos, *dormís*, **duermen**

acordarse	contar	doler	morir
acostarse	costar	encontrar	mostrar
almorzar	devolver	llevar	volver

E to I stem-changing verbs

PEDIR: pido, pides, pide, pedimos, *pedís*, **piden**

corregir	repetir	servir	vestirse
reirse	seguir	sonreir	

Other stem-changing verbs

JUGAR: juego, juegas, juega, jugamos, *jugáis*, **juegan**	**U to UE**
OLER: huelo, hueles, huele, olemos, *olís*, **huelen**	**O to HUE**

PRETERITE TENSE Stem-changing verbs that end in **IR** in the **present tense** also stem-change in the **preterite**. The stem-change only occurs in the third person singular (*he*, *she*, and **usted**), and in the third person plural *(they*, and *you all).*

E changes to I, and O changes to U

PEDIR: pedí, pediste, **pidió,** pedimos, *pedisteis*, **pidieron**
MORIR: morí, moriste, **murió,** morimos, *moristeis*, **murieron**

The Tool Shed

POR & PARA

Por and **para** have a variety of meanings and uses, and learning all cases in which they occur is extremely difficult.

Por can be translated as *for, during, because of, in exchange for, on behalf of, through, by, by means of, along, in the vicinity of,* and others. Below are common categories in which they occur.

GIVE AND TAKE (between people or forces, often indicates a two-way exchange or interaction)

Gracias por su atención.	*Thanks for your attention.*
Juana me lo vendió por cinco pesos.	*Juana sold it to me for five pesos.*
Ellos votaron por Alfredo.	*They voted for Alfredo.*
Nacho murió por no cuidarse.	*Nacho died because he didn't take care of himself.*
Paso por la niña pronto.	*I will pick up the girl soon.*

PREPOSITION (indicating location, or means of travel)

Caminamos por la playa.	*We walk along the beach.* *We walk through the beach.* *We walk by the beach.*
Beto vive por Rosarito.	*Beto lives in the area of Rosarito.*
Voy por tren.	*I go by train.* *I go by means of train.*

MATH AND NUMBERS (including frequency, and length of time)

Dos por cinco son diez.	*Two times five is ten.*
Nado seis veces por semana.	*I swim six times weekly.*
Ella habló por una hora entera.	*She spoke for an entire hour.*

The Tool Shed

GENERAL TIME OF DAY

Trabajo por la mañana.	*I work in the morning.*
Visito a mi mamá por la tarde.	*I visit my mom in the afternoon.*
Ellos salen por la noche.	*They go out in the evening.*

COMMON PHRASES WITH POR

por ejemplo	*for example*
por eso	*for that reason*
por lo general	*in general*
por lo menos	*at least*
por si acaso	*just in case*
por supuesto	*of course*

Para nearly always refers to a goal, destination, or purpose. It is usually translated as *for.*

GOAL, DESTINATION, DEADLINE, INTENDED FOR... This is the most common use of **para**. In these uses, **para** often emphasizes one direction of an exchange.

El regalo es para Ana.	*The gift is for Ana.*
Leo para la clase mañana.	*I'm reading for the class tomorrow.*
Ya salí para Tijuana.	*I already left for Tijuana.*
Pedro trabaja para Josue.	*Pedro works for Josue.*

MAKING COMPARISONS (often implied)

Para mí, ejercicio es difícil.	*For me, exercise is hard.*
Habla muy poco para maestro.	*He speaks very little for a teacher.*

The Tool Shed

PRESENT PROGRESSIVE

When you say *I am* ____, and fill in the blank with a verb ending in *-ing (talking walking, studying)*, you are using the **present progressive**.

Ella está estudiando.	*She is studying.*
Estoy comiendo.	*I am eating.*
Estamos escribiendo.	*We are writing.*

In English, the **present progressive** can be used to refer to the present *(I am jogging)*, or the future *(I am playing golf tomorrow).* In Spanish, the **present progressive** can only be used to describe what is happening at the present time…never for the future!

The **present progressive** is an easy, two-part construction: **estar + present participle** (the **present participle** is the *-ing* form of a verb).

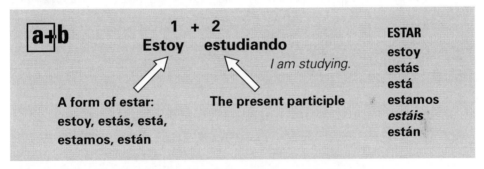

a+b	**1 + 2**
	Estoy estudiando
	I am studying.
	A form of estar: estoy, estás, está, estamos, están
	The present participle

ESTAR
estoy
estás
está
estamos
estáis
están

For regular verbs, the **past participle** is formed as follows:

AR verbs, add -**ando** to the stem:	hablar	habl**ando**
ER verbs, add -**iendo** to the stem:	comer	com**iendo**
IR verbs, add -**iendo** to the stem:	escribir	escrib**iendo**

The Tool Shed

The Tool Shed

The Tool Shed

The Tool Shed

CHAPTER 25

IR stem-changing verbs also change in the present participle: o-u, and e-i.

decir	diciendo	repetir	repitiendo
dormir	durmiendo	sentir	sintiendo
mentir	mintiendo	servir	sirviendo
morir	muriendo	venir	viniendo
pedir	pidiendo	vestir	vistiendo

Some verbs change in the present participle to maintain uniform pronunciation (also known as an orthographic change).

caer	cayendo	ir	yendo
creer	creyendo	oír	oyendo
huir	huyendo	traer	trayendo
influir	influyendo	leer	leyendo

Object and reflexive pronouns can be attached to the end of the present participle. A written accent must be included (the accent falls on the a or the e).

regalándotela	conociéndolos

CHAPTER 26

The Tool Shed

NUMBERS

1-20

1 uno	6 seis	11 once	16 dieciséis
2 dos	7 siete	12 doce	17 diecisiete
3 tres	8 ocho	13 trece	18 dieciocho
4 cuatro	9 nueve	14 catorce	19 diecinueve
5 cinco	10 diez	15 quince	20 veinte

21-29 are one word. The word for twenty, **veinte**, is changed to **veinti** and the second number is added onto the end.

21 veintiuno	24 veinticuatro	27 veintisiete
22 veintidós	25 veinticinco	28 veintiocho
23 veintitrés	26 veintiséis	29 veintinueve

30-99 are all formed similarly. Thirty, forty, fifty, sixty, seventy, eighty, and ninety are all one word (**treinta**, **cuarenta**, etc.). The numbers between 30, 40, 50 (31,32, etc.), are formed using three words (**treinta y uno**, **cuarenta y uno**, etc.).

30 treinta	40 cuarenta	40 cuarenta
31 treinta y uno	41 cuarenta y uno	50 cincuenta
32 treinta y dos	42 cuarenta y dos	60 sesenta
33 treinta y tres	43 cuarenta y tres	70 setenta
34 treinta y cuatro	44 cuarenta y cuatro	80 ochenta
35 treinta y cinco	45 cuarenta y cinco	90 noventa
36 treinta y seis	46 cuarenta y seis	
37 treinta y siete	47 cuarenta y siete	
38 treinta y ocho	48 cuarenta y ocho	
39 treinta y nueve	49 cuarenta y nueve	

100 is one word, **cien**. Starting with the number 101, **cien** changes to **ciento**. To form 101-199, use **ciento** plus the appropriate number. Numbers 200-999 are formed similarly (**doscientos diez**, **trescientos ocho**).

100 cien	200 doscientos	1000 mil
101 ciento uno	300 trescientos	1002 mil dos
102 ciento dos	400 cuatrocientos	1055 mil cincuenta y cinco
103 ciento tres	500 quinientos	
121 ciento veintiuno	600 seiscientos	10,000 diez mil
130 ciento treinta	700 setecientos	100,000 cien mil
142 ciento cuarenta y dos	800 ochocientos	1,000,000 un millón
153 ciento cincuenta y tres	900 novecientos	1,000,000,000 un billón
205 doscientos cinco		

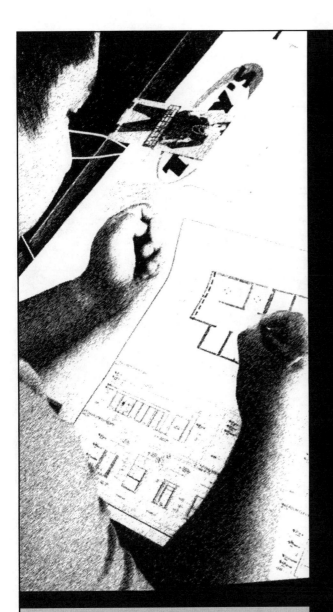

SECTION 5

VOCABULARY
CHAPTERS 25-41

Vocabulary

TAKING A TRIP AND LODGING

People	Verbs (continued)
conductor- **el revisor**	to buy- **comprar**
driver- **el chofer**	to climb (mountains)- **escalar**
flight attendant- **el (la) asistente de vuelo**	to depart- **partir**
flight crew- **la tripulación**	to fall down- **caer(se)**
passenger- **el pasajero**	to go camping- **hacer camping, acampar**
pilot- **el (la) piloto**	to happen- **pasar, suceder**
tour guide- **el (la) guía**	to meet, to know- **conocer**
traveler- **el viajero**	to pack suitcases- **hacer las maletas**
Places	to return (objects)- **devolver (ue)**
cabin (in a ship)- **la cabina**	to ride a horse- **montar a caballo**
campground- **el camping, el campa-mento**	to swim- **nadar**
capital city- **la capital**	to talk on the phone- **hablar por teléfono**
forest- **el bosque**	to tell- **contar (ue)**
garden- **el jardín**	to travel- **viajar**
highway- **la carretera**	to wait in line- **hacer cola**
hotel- **el hotel**	**Associated Words**
house- **la casa**	arrival- **la llegada**
mountain- **la montaña**	binoculars- **los binoculares**
museum- **el museo**	camera- **la cámara fotográfica**
ocean- **el océano**	card- **la tarjeta**
port- **el puerto**	delay- **el retraso, la demora**
river- **el río**	departure, exit- **la salida**
sea- **el mar**	during- **durante**
street- **la calle**	excess- **el exceso**
train station- **la estación de tren**	first class- **la primera clase**
travel agency- **la agencia de viajes**	flight- **el vuelo**
waiting room- **la sala de espera**	hour, time- **la hora**
window, box office- **la vantanilla**	landing- **el aterrizaje**
Verbs	last- **último**
I would like- **me gustaría**	late- **tarde**
to announce- **anunciar**	lodging- **el alojamiento**
to be on vacation- **estar de vacaciones**	long- **largo**

Vocabulary

Associated Words (continued)	Ticketing
luggage- **el equipaje**	one way- **de ida**
mine- **míos, mías**	one way trip- **el viaje sencillo**
monument- **el monumento**	round-trip- **de ida y vuelta**
on a trip- **de viaje**	ticket- **el boleto**
on time- **a tiempo**	**Method of Travel**
photo(graph)- **la foto(grafía)**	bicycle- **la bicicleta**
roll of film- **el rollo de película**	boat, ship- **el barco**
seat- **el asiento, la silla**	bus- **el autobús**
suitcase- **la maleta**	helicopter- **el helicóptero**
the trip- **el viaje**	plane- **el avión**
together- **juntos(as)**	taxi- **el taxi**
tour- **la excursion**	train- **el tren**
view- **la vista**	

Vocabulary

GETTING AROUND ROADS & CITIES

People	Associated Words
driver- **el/la conductor(a)**	*accident-* **el accidente**
mechanic- **el mecánico**	*air-* **el aire**
police- **el policia**	*battery-* **la batería, la pila**
public- **el público**	*beautiful-* **bello, bonito**
Places	*brake-* **el freno**
countryside- **el campo**	*broken-* **descompuesto**
downtown- **el centro**	*corner-* **la esquina**
gas station- **la gasolinera**	*crime-* **el delito**
subway- **el metro**	*engine-* **el motor**
Verbs	*fast-* **acelerado, rápido**
to be located- **quedar, ubicar**	*flat-* **desinflado, ponchado**
to check- **chequear, revisar**	*freeway-* **la autopista**
to conserve- **conservar, preservar**	*full-* **lleno**
to continue- **seguir**	*gasoline-* **la gasolina**
to drive- **conducir, manejar**	*glove compartment-* **la guantera**
to fix- **arreglar**	*highway-* **la carretera**
to give a ticket- **poner una multa**	*license plate-* **la placa**
to have a flat tire- **tener un pinchazo**	*nice-* **amable (for people)**
to hitchhike- **hacer autostop**	*noise-* **el ruido**
to install- **instalar**	*noisy-* **ruidoso**
to obey- **obedecer**	*oil-* **el aceite**
to park- **estacionarse**	*out of order-* **estar descompuesto**
to pollute- **contaminar**	*pollution-* **la contaminación**
to run into- **chocar**	*repair-* **el arreglo, la reparación**
to run out- **acabar**	*service-* **el servicio**
to spend- **gastar**	*shortage-* **la escasez**
to start a car- **arrancar, poner en marcha**	*speed-* **la velocidad**
to stop- **parar**	*speed limit-* **la velocidad máxima**
to try- **tratar (de), intentar**	*strange, funny, odd-* **extraño, raro**
to turn- **doblar**	*tank-* **el tanque**
to waste- **desperdiciar**	*ticket window-* **la ventanilla**
to work- **funcionar**	*tire-* **la llanta, neumático**

Vocabulary

Associated Words (continued)	Directions
traffic- **el tráfico, la caravana**	*across from*- **en frente de**
traffic light- **el semáforo, la luz**	*block*- **la cuadra, la manzana**
water- **el agua**	*east*- **el este**
windshield wiper- **el limpiaparabrisas**	*get going!*- **¡anda!, ¡ándale!**
Method of Travel	*mile*- **la milla**
bicycle- **la bicicleta (la bici)**	*north*- **el norte**
bus- **el autobús**	*sign*- **el letrero, la señal**
motorcycle- **la motocicleta (la moto)**	*south*- **el sur**
tow truck- **la grúa**	*straight ahead*- **derecho**
transportation- **el transporte**	*west*- **el oeste**
truck- **el camión**	

Vocabulary

RESTAURANT & FOOD

People	Fruits & Vegetables
chef- **el chef**	apple- **la manzana**
cook- **el cocinero**	banana- **el plátano**
butcher- **el carnicero**	beans- **los frijoles**
waiter- **el camarero, el mesero**	carrot- **la zanahoria**
Places	grape- **la uva**
bakery- **la panadería**	lemon- **el limón**
kitchen- **la cocina**	lettuce- **la lechuga**
market- **el mercado**	orange- **la naranja**
supermarket- **el supermercado**	pear- **la pera**
Verbs	potato- **la papa**
to be on a diet- **estar a dieta**	salad- **la ensalada**
to boil- **hervir (ie)**	strawberry- **la fresa**
to cut- **cortar**	vegetable- **la verdura, el legumbre**
to invite- **invitar**	**Meat & Poultry**
to mix- **mezclar**	beef- **la carne de res**
to pay- **pagar**	pork- **el puerco, las carnitas**
to prepare- **preparar**	chicken- **el pollo**
to snack- **merendar**	egg- **el huevo**
to wait for- **esperar**	fish- **el pescado**
to weigh- **pesar**	hamburger- **la hamburguesa**
Food	meat- **la carne**
bread- **el pan**	turkey- **el pavo**
candy- **los dulces**	**Drinks**
cereal- **el cereal**	beer- **la cerveza**
cheese- **el queso**	coffee- **el café**
corn- **el maíz**	juice- **el jugo**
ice cream- **el helado, la nieve (snow)**	milk- **la leche**
mushroom- **el champiñón**	soft drink- **el refresco, la soda**
rice- **el arroz**	tea- **el té**
soup- **la sopa**	wine- **el vino**
toast- **el pan tostado**	**Kitchen Utensils**
	fork- **el tenedor**

Vocabulary

Kitchen Utensils (continued)	Associated Words (continued)
glass, cup- **el vaso, la taza**	*healthy-* **sano**
knife- **el cuchillo**	*hot (temp-* **caliente**
plate- **el plato**	*lunch-* **el almuerzo**
spoon- **la cuchara**	*menu-* **el menú**
Associated Words	*olive oil-* **el aceite de olivo**
bottle- **la botella**	*order-* **el pedido, la orden**
check, bill- **la cuenta**	*pound-* **la libra**
course, dish- **el plato**	*price-* **el precio**
delicious- **delicioso, sabroso, rico**	*roasted-* **asado**
dessert- **el postre**	*salt-* **la sal**
dinner- **la cena**	*sugar-* **el azúcar**
dozen- **la docena**	*sweet-* **dulce**
fat- **gordo**	*tasty-* **sabroso**
fried- **frito**	*tip-* **la propina, el servicio**
greasy- **grasoso**	

Vocabulary

FAMILY & HOME

People	Verbs
aunt- **la tía**	to add (not math)- **añadir, agregar**
boy- **el chico, el muchacho**	to bake- **hornear**
boyfriend- **el novio**	to bathe (oneself)- **bañar(se)**
brother- **el hermano**	to beat- **batir**
child- **el niño**	to cook- **cocinar**
cousin- **el primo**	to finish- **terminar**
dad- **el papá, el padre**	to get dressed- **vestirse (i)**
daughter- **la hija**	to get up- **levantarse**
father- **el padre**	to go shopping- **ir de compras**
girl- **la chica, la muchacha**	to go to bed- **acostarse (ue)**
girlfriend- **la novia**	to heat up- **calentar**
grandfather- **el abuelo**	to iron- **planchar**
grandmother- **la abuela**	to live- **vivir**
husband- **el esposo**	to mix- **mezclar**
man- **el hombre**	to move- **mudarse**
parents- **los padres**	to open- **abrir**
sister- **la hermana**	to put on- **ponerse**
uncle- **el tío**	to sweep- **barrer**
wife- **la esposa**	to vacuum- **pasar la aspiradora**
woman- **la mujer**	to wear- **llevar**
Places In the Home	**Kitchen Items**
bedroom- **el dormitorio, el cuarto**	dishwasher- **el lavaplatos**
dining room- **el comedor**	freezer- **el congelador**
garage- **el garaje**	frying pan- **el/la sartén**
kitchen- **la cocina**	oven- **el horno**
living room- **la sala**	refrigerator- **el refrigerador**
Places Outside the Home	silverware- **los cubiertos**
apartment- **el apartamento, el departamento**	sink- **el fregadero, el lavabo**
garden- **el jardín**	stove- **la estufa**
house- **la casa**	toaster- **la tostadora**
neighborhood- **el barrio, la vecindad**	**Associated Words**
	air conditioning- **el aire acondicionado**

Vocabulary

Associated Words (continued)	Associated Words (continued)
blanket- **la manta, la cobija**	*purse-* **el bolso**
blouse- **la blusa**	*rent-* **el alquiler**
carpet- **la alfombra**	*shirt-* **la camisa**
chair- **la silla**	*shoe-* **el zapato**
clean- **limpio**	*skirt-* **la falda**
dirty- **sucio**	*socks-* **los calcetines**
furniture- **los muebles**	*sofa-* **el sofá**
gloves- **los guantes**	*stairs-* **la escalera**
jacket- **la chaqueta, la chamarra**	*suit-* **el traje**
mirror- **el espejo**	*vacuum cleaner-* **la aspiradora**
pillow- **la almohada**	

Vocabulary

DAILY ROUTINE

Places	Verbs
bookstore- **la librería**	*to call-* **llamar**
gym- **el gimnasio**	*to chat-* **charlar**
library- **la biblioteca**	*to die-* **morirse**
movie theater- **el cine**	*to do-* **hacer**
Inside the Home (Verbs)	*to finish-* **acabar, terminar**
to brush- **cepillarse**	*to get angry-* **enojarse**
to brush one's teeth- **cepillarse los dientes**	*to make-* **hacer**
to drink- **tomar, beber**	*to practice-* **practicar**
to eat- **comer**	*to prepare-* **preparer**
to get dressed- **vestirse (i)**	*to return-* **regresar, volver (ue)**
to get up- **levantarse**	*to smoke-* **fumar**
to go to bed- **acostarse (ue)**	*to speak, talk-* **hablar**
to have lunch- **almorzar**	*to spend time-* **pasar tiempo**
to put on makeup- **maquillarse**	*to study-* **estudiar**
to shave- **afeitarse**	*to think-* **pensar (ie)**
to sleep- **dormir**	*to use-* **usar, utilizar**
to take a bath- **bañarse**	*to want-* **desear, querer (ie)**
to take a nap- **dormir (ue) la siesta**	*to wear-* **llevar**
to take a shower- **ducharse**	**Hygiene & Maintenance**
to wake up- **despertarse (ie)**	*brush-* **el cepillo**
Outside the Home (verbs)	*comb-* **el peine**
to buy- **comprar**	*deodorant-* **el desodorante**
to dance- **bailar**	*hair dryer-* **la secadora**
to exercise- **hacer ejercicio**	*makeup-* **el maquillaje**
to go- **ir**	*mouthwash-* **el enjuague bucal**
to go away- **irse**	*razor-* **la navaja de afeitar**
to have a good time- **divertirse (ie)**	*shampoo-* **el champú**
to mail a letter- **mandar una carta**	*shaving cream-* **la crema de afeitar**
to sunbathe- **tomar el sol**	*soap-* **el jabón**
to take a trip- **hacer un viaje**	*toothpaste-* **la pasta dental**
to travel- **viajar**	**The Body**
to work- **trabajar**	*arm-* **el brazo**

Vocabulary

The Body (continued)	Associated Words (continued)
body- **el cuerpo**	*during-* **durante**
face- **la cara**	*early-* **temprano**
fingers- **los dedos**	*early riser-* **el/la madrugador(a)**
foot- **el pie**	*friend-* **el amigo**
hands- **las manos**	*homework-* **la tarea**
head- **la cabeza**	*late-* **atrasado, tarde**
leg- **la pierna**	*mirror-* **el espejo**
mouth- **la boca**	*money-* **el dinero**
stomach- **el estómago**	*roommate-* **el compañero de cuarto**
teeth- **los dientes**	*swimming pool-* **la piscina, la alberca**
Associated Words	*today-* **hoy**
all day- **todo el día**	*toothbrush-* **el cepillo de dientes**
bedroom- **el dormitorio, el cuarto**	*towel-* **la toalla**
daily routine- **la rutina diaria**	*weekend-* **el fin de semana**
dining room- **el comedor**	

Vocabulary

SPORTS & GAMES

People	Verbs (continued)
boxer- **el/la boxeador(a)**	to throw- **tirar**
champion- **el/la campeón(a)**	to pitch- **lanzar**
cyclist- **el/la ciclista**	to train- **entrenar**
fan- **el aficionado**	to win- **ganar**
player- **el/la jugador(a)**	to win, beat- **ganar, vencer**
swimmer- **el/la nadador(a)**	**Associated Words**
tennis player- **el/la tenista**	active- **activo**
trainer, coach- **el/la entrenador(a)**	ball- **la pelota**
Places	bat- **el bate**
baseball field- **el campo de béisbol**	championship- **el campeonato**
soccer field- **el campo de fútbol**	competition- **la competencia**
stadium- **el estadio**	congratulations!- **¡felicidades!**
swimming pool- **la piscina, la alberca**	dominos- **el dominó**
tennis court- **la cancha de tennis**	equipment- **el eqiuipaje**
Verbs	event- **el evento**
to ski- **esquiar**	exercise- **los ejercicios**
to surf- **surfear**	force, strength- **la fuerza**
to swim- **nadar**	free time- **los ratos libres**
to bat- **batear**	game, match- **el partido**
to catch- **atrapar**	glove- **el guante**
to fight- **pelear**	injured- **lastimado**
to harm- **dañar(se), lastimar(se)**	net- **la red**
to hit- **pegar**	olympics- **las olipiadas**
to improve, get better- **mejorar**	race- **la carrera**
to kick- **golpear con el pie**	racket- **la raqueta**
to lose- **perder (ie)**	rule- **la regla**
to play- **jugar(ue)**	score- **el tanto**
to ride a bike- **montar en bicicleta**	season- **la temporada**
to ride a horse- **montar a caballo**	skis- **los esquís**
to run- **correr**	strong- **fuerte**
to skate- **patinar**	team- **el equipo**
to ski- **esquiar**	uniform- **el uniforme**
to take a walk- **dar un paseo/ una veulta**	weak- **débil**

Vocabulary

Individual Sports	Individual Sports (continued)
bowling- **el boliche**	*track and field-* **el atletismo**
cycling- **el ciclismo**	*water skiing-* **el esquí acuático**
fishing- **la pesca**	*wrestling-* **la lucha grecorromana**
golf- **el golf**	**Team Sports**
gymnastics- **la gimnasia**	*baseball-* **el béisbol**
jogging- **correr**	*basketball-* **el básquetbol**
karate- **el kárate**	*football-* **el fútbol americano**
marathon- **el maratón**	*hockey-* **el hockey**
mountain climbing- **el alpinismo**	*soccer-* **el fútbol**
skiing- **el esquí**	*softball-* **el sofból**
surfing- **el surfing**	*volleyball-* **el volibol**
swimming- **la natación**	*waterpolo-* **el polo acuático**
tennis- **el tenis**	

Vocabulary

CHAPTER 33

ART & CULTURE

People	Associated Words (continued)
actor, actress- **el actor, la actriz**	*I hope*- **ojalá**
architect- **el arquitecto**	*incredible*- **increíble**
composer- **el/la compositor(a)**	*masterpiece*- **la obra maestra**
dancer- **el bailarín/la bailarina**	*modern*- **moderno**
director- **el/la director(a)**	*movie*- **la película**
musician- **el músico**	*music*- **la música**
painter- **el/la pintor(a)**	*painting*- **el cuadro**
poet- **el/la poeta**	*playwright*- **el dramaturgo**
sculptor- **el/la escultor(a)**	*role*- **el papel**
singer- **el/la cantante**	*script*- **el guión**
writer- **el/la escritor(a)**	*song*- **la canción**
Verbs	*strange*- **extraño, raro**
it bothers me- **me molesta**	*work of art*- **la obra de arte**
it surprises me- **me suprende**	**Art**
to paint- **pintar**	*art*- **el arte**
to appreciate- **apreciar**	*arts and crafts*- **la artesanía**
it bores me- **me aburre**	*painting*- **la pintura**
to draw- **dibujar**	*pottery*- **la cerámica**
to please- **agradar**	*sculpture*- **la escultura**
to represent- **representar**	**Cultural Events & Places**
to sculpt- **esculpir**	*ballet*- **el ballet**
to see- **ver**	*concert*- **el concierto**
to seem- **parecer**	*cultural event*- **una diversión cultural**
to try- **intentar**	*dance (event)*- **el baile**
to try to- **tratar de + inf.**	*exposition, showing*- **la exposición**
to weave- **tejer**	*movie theater*- **el cine**
Associated Words	*museum*- **el museo**
architecture- **la arquitectura**	*opera*- **la ópera**
classic- **clásico**	*presentation*- **la presentación**
excellent- **excelente**	*stage*- **el escenario**
fantastic- **fantástico**	*theater*- **el teatro**
folkloric- **folklórico**	

Vocabulary

HEALTH & MEDICINE

People	Verbs (continued)
doctor- **el doctor**	*to stay in shape-* **mantenerse en forma**
nurse- **la enfermera**	*to suffer-* **sufrir**
patient- **el/la paciente**	*to take care of-* **cuidar**
pharmacist- **el farmacéutico**	*to weigh-* **pesar**
Places	**Associated Words**
clinic- **la clínica**	*alcohol-* **el alcohol**
doctor's office- **el consultorio, la consulta**	*allergic-* **alérgico**
emergency room- **la sala de emergencia**	*ambulance-* **la ambulancia**
health store- **la tienda naturalista**	*analysis-* **el análisis**
hospital- **el hospital**	*antibiotics-* **los antibióticos**
pharmacy- **la farmacia**	*as soon as possible-* **lo más pronto posible**
Verbs	*cheer up!-* **¡más ánimo!**
to bandage- **vendar**	*cholesterol-* **el colesterol**
to be on a diet- **estar a dieta**	*cigarette--* **el cigarillo**
to bleed- **sangrar**	*disease-* **la enfermedad**
to break- **romper**	*dizzy-* **mareado**
to complain- **quejarse**	*eyesight-* **la vista**
to control- **controlar**	*headache-* **dolor de cabeza**
to cough- **toser**	*healthy-* **saludable**
to cure- **curar**	*height-* **la estatura**
to die- **morir**	*medicine-* **la medicina**
to discover- **descubrir**	*nauseated-* **mareado**
to gain weight- **aumentar de peso**	*overweight-* **sobrepeso**
to get sick- **enfermarse**	*pain-* **el dolor**
to get well- **sanar**	*painful-* **doloroso**
to give an injection- **poner una inyección**	*pill-* **la pastilla**
to limit- **limitar**	*pregnant-* **embarazada**
to lose weight- **adelgazar**	*protein-* **la proteína**
to prescribe- **recetar**	*serious-* **grave, serio**
to reduce- **reducir**	*sick-* **enfermo**
to rest- **descansar**	*sickness-* **el enfermedad**
to run- **correr**	*suddenly-* **de repente**

Vocabulary

Associated Words (Continued)	Body (continued)
temperature- **la temperatura**	*face-* **la cara**
treatment- **el tratamiento**	*foot-* **el pie**
weight- **el peso**	*hair-* **el pelo**
wound- **la herida**	*hand-* **la mano**
Body	*heart-* **el corazón**
arm- **el brazo**	*leg-* **la pierna**
back- **la espalda**	*lips-* **los labios**
blood- **la sangre**	*mouth-* **la boca**
bone- **el hueso**	*muscle-* **el músculo**
brain- **el cerebro**	*nose-* **la nariz**
chest- **el pecho**	*skeleton-* **el esqueleto**
cranium- **el cráneo**	*skin-* **la piel**
ear- **la oreja**	*stomach-* **el estómago**
eye- **el ojo**	*teeth-* **los dientes**

Vocabulary

SOCIAL LIFE

Romance	Verbs (continued)
at first sight- **a primera vista**	*to take-* **tomar**
boyfriend- **el novio**	*to toast-* **brindar**
to break up with- **romper con**	*to want-* **querer**
divorce- **el divorcio**	**Associated Words**
engagement- **el noviazgo**	*bar-* **el bar, la cantina**
to fall in love- **enamorarse**	*because-* **porque**
to get divorced- **divorciarse**	*beer-* **la cerveza**
girlfriend- **la novia**	*busy-* **ocupado**
honeymoon- **la luna de miel**	*champagne-* **el champán**
love- **el amor**	*cider-* **la sidra**
to love- **amar**	*classmate-* **compañero de clase**
to love, to want- **querer (ie)**	*club-* **el club**
marriage- **el matrimonio**	*cocktail-* **el coctel**
to marry- **casarse**	*compact disc-* **el disco compacto**
wedding- **la boda**	*dance-* **el baile**
Verbs	*drink-* **la bebida**
I'm hot- **tengo calor**	*enough-* **bastante**
I'm hungry- **tengo hambre**	*everybody-* **todos(as), todo el mundo**
I'm thirsty- **tengo sed**	*friend-* **el amigo**
shall we dance?- **¿bailamos?**	*friendly-* **amistoso**
to be born- **nacer**	*friendship-* **la amistad**
to begin- **empezar (ie)**	*great-* **magnífico**
to bring- **traer**	*happy-* **feliz**
to celebrate- **celebrar**	*hors d'oeuvres-* **los entremeses**
to dance- **bailar**	*house-* **la casa**
to give- **dar**	*idea-* **la idea**
to go- **ir**	*midnight-* **la medianoche**
to go away- **irse**	*much, a lot of-* **mucho**
to go out with- **salir con**	*new-* **nuevo**
to grow- **crecer**	*salad-* **la ensalada**
to invite- **invitar**	*soda-* **el refresco, la soda**
to spend time- **pasar tiempo**	*stereo-* **el estéreo**
to start- **comenzar (ie)**	*terrace-* **la terraza**

Vocabulary

Associated Words (continued)	Celebrations (continued)
tired- **cansado**	*party-* **la fiesta**
together- **juntos(as)**	**Stages of Life**
wine- **el vino**	*adolescence-* **la adolescencia**
young person- **el/la joven**	*birth-* **el nacimiento**
Celebrations	*death-* **la muerte**
birthday – **el cumpleaños**	*maturity-* **la madurez**
christmas party- **la fiesta de navidad**	*old age-* **la vejez**
new years eve party- **fiesta de año nuevo**	*youth-* **la juventud**

Vocabulary

POLITICS & THE MEDIA

People	Associated Words (continued)
citizen- **el ciudadano**	comic strip- **la tira cómica**
commentator- **el comentarista**	congress- **el congreso**
critic- **el crítico**	crime- **el crimen**
governor- **el gobernador**	death penalty- **la pena de muerte**
journalist- **el periodista**	democracy- **la democracia**
judge- **el/la juez**	development- **el desarrollo**
king- **el rey**	dictatorship- **la dictadura**
mayor- **el/la alcalde(sa)**	doubtful- **dudoso**
president- **el/la presidente(a)**	duty--**el deber**
queen- **la reina**	election- **la elección**
reporter- **el reportero**	environment- **el medio ambiente**
show host- **el anfitrión**	event, happening- **el acontecimiento**
the people, masses--**el pueblo**	government- **el gobierno**
weatherman- **el meteorólogo**	horoscope- **el horóscopo**
Verbs	important- **importante**
let's vote!- **¡a votar!**	inflation- **la inflación**
let's win!- **¡a ganar!**	law- **la ley**
to cover- **cubrir**	monarchy- **la monarquía**
to elect, choose- **elegir**	obituary- **la necrología, la esquela mortuoria**
to fight, combat- **combatir**	opponent- **el/la contrincante**
to find out- **enterarse**	political party- **el partido político**
to get worse- **empeorar**	poll- **la encuesta**
to ignore- **ignorer**	pollution- **la contaminación**
to improve- **mejorar**	priority- **la prioridad**
to resolve- **resolver**	senate- **el senato**
to sacrifice- **sacrificar**	speech- **el discurso**
to support- **apoyar**	strange- **extraño, raro**
to triumph- **triunfar**	survey- **la encuesta**
to vote- **votar**	taxes- **los impuestos**
Associated Words	the majority- **la mayoría**
assault- **el asalto**	**News**
campaign- **la campaña**	article- **el artículo**
classified ads- **los avisos clasificados**	channel- **el canal**

News (continued)	*news, story-* **la crónica**
editorial page- **el editorial**	*newscast-* **el noticiero**
headline- **el titular**	*press-* **la prensa**
live television- **en vivo**	*radio station-* **la emisora**
magazine- **la revista**	*review-* **la reseña**
news- **las noticias**	

CHAPTER 37

Vocabulary

WORK & PROFESSIONS

Group 1	Group 2 (continued)
athlete- **el/la atleta**	*musician-* **el músico**
babysitter- **el/la niñera**	*nurse-* **el enfermero**
bartender- **el tabernero, el barman**	*programmer-* **el/la programador(a)**
beautician- **el peluquero**	*salesperson-* **el/la vendedor(a)**
butcher- **el carnicero**	*teacher-* **el maestro**
coach- **el/la entrenador(a)**	**Group 3**
contractor- **el/la contratista**	*anthropologist-* **el antropólogo**
cook- **el cocinero**	*archaeologist-* **el arqueólogo**
electrician- **el/la electricista**	*architect-* **el arquitecto**
gardener- **el jardinero**	*astronaut-* **el/la astronauta**
hair stylist- **el peluquero**	*attorney-* **el abogado**
housewife- **la ama de casa**	*banker-* **el banquero**
janitor- **el/la conserje**	*C.E.O.-* **el/la director(a)**
laborer- **el obrero**	*chemist-* **el químico**
lifeguard- **el/la salvavidas**	*dentist-* **el/la dentista**
mechanic- **el mecánico**	*doctor-* **el/la doctor(a)**
minister- **el ministro**	*judge-* **el/la juez**
waiter- **el camarero, el mesero**	*pilot-* **el piloto**
Group 2	*pharmacist-* **el farmacéutico**
actor- **el actor/la actriz**	**Verbs**
announcer- **el anunciador**	*to attend-* **asistir a**
artist- **el/la artista**	*to change-* **cambiar**
author- **el/la autor(a)**	*to decide-* **decidir**
barber- **el barbero**	*to open-* **abrir**
cop- **el/la policía**	*to receive-* **recibir**
counselor- **el consejero**	*to sell-* **vender**
dealer- **el/la vendedor(a)**	*to write-* **escribir**
detective- **el detective**	**Associated Words**
firefighter- **el bombero**	*appointment-* **la cita**
instructor- **el/la instructor(a)**	*apprentice-* **el/la aprendiz(a)**
journalist- **el/la periodista**	*assistant-* **el/la asistente**
librarian- **el bibliotecario**	*boring-* **aburrido(a)**
manager- **el/la gerente**	*boss-* **el/la jefe(a)**

Assiciated Words (continued)	Assiciated Words (continued)
career- **la carrera**	*leader*- **el/la líder**
company, *firm*- **la compañía**	*job*- **el trabajo, el empleo**
employee- **el empleado**	*salary*- **el salario**
expert- **el experto**	*schedule*- **el horario**
hardworking- **aplicado, trabajador(a)**	*store*- **la tienda**
interview- **la entrevista**	*student*- **el/la estudiante**
lazy- **perezoso, flojo**	

Vocabulary

SCHOOL

People	Associated Words (continued)
classmate- **el compañero de clase**	boring- **aburrido**
counselor- **el consejero**	calculator- **la calculadora**
librarian- **el bibliotecario**	career- **la carrera**
principal- **el/la director(a)**	class schedule- **el horario de clases**
professor- **el/la profesor(a)**	complicated- **complicado**
student- **el/la estudiante**	course- **el curso**
teacher- **el maestro**	day- **el día**
Verbs	desk- **el escritorio, el pupitre**
to go on foot- **ir a pie**	dictionary- **el diccionario**
to be successful- **tener éxito**	difficult- **difícil**
to fail- **aprobar(ue), perder(ie)**	discussion- **la discusión**
to get a grade- **sacar una nota**	door- **la puerta**
to graduate- **graduarse**	easy- **fácil**
to help- **ayudar**	every day- **todos los días**
to listen- **escuchar**	grade- **la nota**
to maintain- **mantener**	grade point average- **el promedio**
to play- **jugar(ue)**	interesting- **interesante**
to register- **matricularse**	chalkboard- **la pizarra**
to study- **estudiar**	language- **el idioma**
to suppose- **suponer**	late- **tarde**
to turn in- **entregar**	literature- **la literatura**
Places	major- **la especialización**
bookstore- **la librería**	microscope- **el microscopio**
cafeteria- **la cafetería**	notebook- **el cuaderno**
gymnasium- **el gimnasio**	paper- **el papel**
classroom- **la sala de clase, la clase**	pen- **el bolígrafo, la pluma**
library- **la biblioteca**	pencil- **el lápiz**
student center- **el centro estudiantil**	poorly- **mal**
university- **la universidad**	quarter- **el trimestre**
Associated Words	report- **el informe**
advice- **el consejo**	requirement- **el requisito**
backpack- **la mochila**	research- **la investigación**

Vocabulary

Associated Words (continued)	Classes
scholarship- **la beca**	algebra- **el álgebra**
school bus- **el bus escolar**	see you later- **hasta luego**
semester- **el semestre**	biology- **la biología**
subject- **la materia**	chemistry- **la química**
table- **la mesa**	economics- **la economía**
team- **el equipo**	history- **la historia**
textbook- **el libro de texto**	math- **las matemáticas**
tuition- **la matricula**	music- **la música**
weekend- **el fin de semana**	physics- **la física**
window- **la ventana**	psychology- **la psicología**
	sociology- **la sociología**

Vocabulary

CLOTHES

Summer	Under Garments (continued)
bathing suit- **el traje de baño, el bañador**	*underwear*- **los calzones**
sandals- **las sandalias**	**Materials & Prints**
Winter	*cotton*- **el algodón**
boots- **las botas**	*gold*- **el oro**
coat- **el abrigo**	*leather*- **el cuero, la piel**
jacket- **la chaqueta, la chamarra**	*plaid*- **de cuadros**
overcoat- **el abrigo**	*polka-dotted*- **de lunares**
scarf- **la bufanda**	*silk*- **la seda**
Active Clothes	*striped*- **de rayas**
blouse- **la blusa**	*wool*- **la lana**
custom made suit- **el traje a la medida**	**Accessories**
dress- **el vestido**	*belt*- **el cinto, el cinturón**
jeans- **los jeans**	*bracelet*- **la pulsera**
long sleeve- **de manga larga**	*earrings*- **los aretes**
overalls- **los pecheros**	*gloves*- **los guantes**
pants- **los pantalones**	*hat*- **el sombrero**
raincoat- **el impermeable**	*necklace*- **el collar**
shirt- **la camisa**	*purse*- **el bolso**
short sleeve- **de manga corta**	*ring*- **el anillo**
shorts- **los pantalones cortos**	*tie*- **la corbata**
skirt- **la falda**	*wallet*- **la billetera, la cartera**
suspenders- **los tirantes de pantalones**	*watch*- **el reloj**
undershirt- **la camiseta**	**Verbs**
vest- **el chaleco**	*how much does it cost?*- **¿cuánto cuesta?**
Under Garments	*to bargain*- **regatear**
boxer shorts- **los calzones**	*to borrow*- **pedir prestado**
bra- **el sostén**	*to go shopping*- **ir de compras**
briefs- **los calzoncillos**	*to match, go well*- **hacer juego**
under garments- **la ropa interior**	*to pay for*- **pagar**
pajamas- **el pijama**	*to return something*- **devolver (ue)**
socks- **los calcetines**	*to want*- **querer (ie)**
stockings- **las medias**	*measurement*- **la medida**
t-shirt- **la camiseta**	*to wear*- **llevar**

Vocabulary

Associated Words	Associated Words (continued)
cash register- **la caja**	*label-* **la etiqueta**
clearance- **liquidación**	*receipt-* **el recibo**
clothing section- **la sección de ropa**	*shoes-* **los zapatos**
department store- **el almacen**	*size-* **la talla**
discount, sale- **la rebaja, la oferta**	*tailor shop-* **la sastrería**
fashion, style- **la moda**	*tennis shoes-* **los zapatos de tenis**
hat shop- **la sombrerería**	*the latest style-* **de última moda**

Vocabulary

ESSENTIAL WORDS

1 Letter	4 Letters (continued)
a- *to*	**solo-** *single, sole, alone*
y- *and*	**sólo-** *only, just*
o- *or*	**5 or More**
2 Letters	**afuera-** *outside*
de- *of, from*	**ahora-** *now*
en- *in, on, at*	**ahorita-** *right now*
si- *if*	**ahora mismo-** *at this moment*
sí- *yes*	**a la derecha-** *to the right*
ya- *already, now*	**alguien-** *someone*
3 Letters	**algún, alguno/a-** *any, some*
acá- *over here*	**a la izquierda-** *to the left*
con- *with*	**al lado de-** *along side*
hay- *there is, there are*	**antes de-** *before*
hoy- *today*	**a tiempo-** *on time*
sin- *without*	**atrasado-** *delayed*
oye- *listen*	**a veces-** *sometimes*
que- *what*	**bastante-** *quite, enough*
por- *for, through, in place of*	**bueno-** *good*
más- *more*	**conmigo-** *with me*
4 Letters	**contigo-** *with you*
algo- *something*	**demasiado-** *too much*
allá- *over there*	**después de-** *after*
allí- *there*	**durante-** *during*
aquí- *here*	**encima de-** *on top of*
bien- *well*	**en frente de-** *facing*
cada- *each*	**en seguida-** *right away*
casi- *almost*	**entonces-** *therefore*
nada- *nothing*	**había-** *there was, there were*
poco- *few*	**igual-** *equal*
para- *for*	**juntos/as-** *together*
pero- *but*	**mañana-** *tomorrow*
pues- *well*	**menos-** *less*

Vocabulary

5 or More (continued)	5 or More (continued)
mucho- *a lot*	**solamente-** *only*
nunca- *never*	**tal vez-** *perhaps*
nunca unca- *never ever*	**también-** *also*
otros/a/os/as- *other*	**tampoco-** *neither*
por eso- *for this/that reason*	**tarde-** *late*
por lo menos- *at least*	**todavía-** *still*
porque- *because*	**todavía no-** *not yet*
quizás- *perhaps*	**todo/a/os/as-** *all, every one*
según- *according to*	**verdad-** *true*
siempre- *always*	**¿verdad?-** *true?, right?*
sin embargo- *however*	

Vocabulary

MOST COMMON VERBS

abrir- to open	**esperar**- to wait, to hope
aceptar- to accept	**explicar**- to explain
amar- to love	**fumar**- to smoke
apagar- to turn off	**ganar**- to win, earn
aprender- to learn	**gastar**- to spend
ayudar- to help	**hablar**- to talk
bailar- to dance	**hacer**- to do/make
beber- to drink	**irse**- to go away
buscar- to look for	**ir**- to go
caerse- to fall	**lavar**- to wash
cambiar- to change	**lavarse**- to wash oneself
cantar- to sing	**leer**- to read
comenzar (ie)- to start/begin	**limpiar**- to clean
comer- to eat	**mirar**- to look at
comprar- to buy	**necesitar**- to need
contar (ue)- to count	**nadar**- to swim
correr- to run	**ocurrir**- to occur
cortar- to cut	**olvidar**- to forget
conducir- to drive	**oír**- to hear
creer- to believe	**pagar**- to pay
dar- to give	**parar**- to stop
deber- to have to/should, to owe	**pedir (i)**- to ask for
decir- to say or tell	**perder (ie)**- to lose
dejar, permitir- to allow	**preguntar**- to ask (a question)
describir- to describe	**prender**- to turn on
despertarse (ie)- to wake up	**pensar (ie)**- to think
dormir (ue)- to sleep	**preparar**- to prepare
dormirse (ue)- to fall asleep	**recibir**- to receive
econtrar (ue)- to find	**romper**- to break
escuchar- to listen	**tener**- to have
estudiar- to study	**temer**- to fear
enseñar- to teach	**terminar**- to finish, to end
entender (ie)- to understand	**tomar**- to take
entrar- to enter	**trabajar**- to work

Vocabulary

traducir- *to translate*	**vender**- *to sell*
traer- *to bring*	**viajar**- *to travel*
usar- *to use*	**vivir**- *to live*
ver- *to see*	

Vocabulary

COGNATES: INSTANT VOCABULARY

action- **la acción**	energy- **la energía**
admirable- **admirable**	equal- **igual**
aggression- **la agresion**	excellent- **excelente**
agriculture- **la agricultura**	expression- **expresión**
ambitious- **ambicioso**	famous- **famoso**
American- **americano**	fantastic- **fantástico**
amiable- **amable**	favorite- **favorito**
anatomy- **la anatomía**	figure- **la figura**
animal- **el animal**	final- **el final**
anniversary- **el aniversario**	geography- **la geografía**
artist- **el/la artista**	honest- **honesto**
attention- **la atención**	horrible- **horrible**
canal- **el canal**	illegal- **ilegal**
central- **central**	impatient- **impaciente**
clear- **claro**	impossible- **imposible**
comfortable- **comfortable**	incorrect- **incorrecto**
comical- **cómico**	indication- **la indicación**
constant- **constante**	innocent- **inocente**
content- **contento**	irresponsible- **irresponsable**
correct- **correcto**	literature- **la literatura**
creative- **creativo**	logic- **la lógica**
cruel- **cruel**	magnificent- **magnífico**
cure- **la cura**	metal- **el metal**
delicious- **delicioso**	miserable- **miserable**
democracy- **la democracia**	monument- **el monumento**
dependent- **dependiente**	music- **la música**
depression- **la depresión**	nationality- **la nacionalidad**
diagram- **el diagrama**	palace- **el palacio**
director- **el/la director(a)**	pharmacy- **la farmacia**
discipline- **la disciplina**	possible- **posible**
drama- **el drama**	problem- **el problema**
electricity- **la electricidad**	program- **el programa**
electronics- **la electrónica**	religious- **religioso**
empty, vacuous- **vacío**	responsible- **responsable**

Vocabulary

ridiculous- **ridículo**	*system-* **el sistema**
significant- **significante**	*tardy-* **tarde**
sincere- **sincero**	*tasty, savory-* **sabroso**
special- **especial**	*terrible-* **terrible**
sufficient- **suficiente**	*tourist-* **el/la turista**
superior- **superior**	*university-* **la universidad**
suspicious- **sospechoso**	*used-* **usado**

Vocabulary

ADJECTIVES

absurd- **absurdo**	good- **bueno**
angry, mad- **enojado**	guilty- **culpable**
annoyed- **enfadado**	handsome- **guapo**
another- **otro**	happy- **alegre**
anxious- **ansioso**	high, tall- **alto**
bad, mean- **malo**	hot- **caliente**
beautiful- **bello, bonito**	illegal- **ilegal**
bitter- **amargo**	impatient- **impaciente**
blind- **ciego**	inexpensive- **barato**
boring- **aburrido**	intelligent- **inteligente**
broken- **roto, descompuesto**	interesting- **interesante**
clean- **limpio**	jealous- **celoso**
clear- **claro**	late- **tardy**
comfortable- **confortable, cómodo**	lazy- **perezoso**
common- **común**	loose- **suelto**
content- **contento**	lost- **perdido**
current- **actual**	loving- **cariñoso**
daily- **cotidiano**	made- **hecho**
dangerous- **peligroso**	married- **casado**
dirty- **sucio**	Mexican- **mexicano**
dishonest- **deshonesto**	filthy- **cochino**
dumb- **tonto**	naughty- **travieso**
early- **temprano**	new- **nuevo**
edible- **comestible**	nude, naked- **desnudo**
excellent- **excelente**	old- **viejo**
expensive- **caro**	painful- **doloroso**
fast- **rápido**	poisonous- **venenoso**
fragile- **frágil**	positive- **positivo**
free- **libre, gratis (no charge)**	quiet- **callado**
friendly- **amable**	roasted- **asado**
full- **lleno**	sad- **triste**
fun- **divertido**	same- **igual**
funny- **cómico**	scared- **asustado**
gentle- **tierno**	severe- **severo**

Vocabulary

short- **corto (opp. of long), bajo (stature), chaparro (stature)**	*ugly-* **feo**
shy- **tímido**	*unique-* **único**
sick- **enfermo**	*useful-* **útil**
sour- **ágrio**	*useless-* **inútil**
special- **especial**	*vulgar-* **vulgar**
stinky- **apestoso**	*weak-* **débil**
surprising- **sorprendente**	*wet-* **mojado**
tired- **cansado**	*wise-* **sabio**

Glossary of Terms

1. **Adjective**: a word that describes a noun. In the phrase, "pretty house," "pretty" is the adjective and "house" is the noun.

2. **Adverb**: an adverb usually modifies a verb. In the phrase "John walks slowly," "slowly" is the adverb. In English, adverbs often end in "ly." In Spanish, adverbs often end in **mente**.

3. **Cognate**: words that are similar in spelling and meaning across languages. For example, **poema** and "poem" are cognates in Spanish and English.

4. **Conjugating**: changing a verb to reflect the subject (the person or thing doing the action). In the phrase "He eats candy," "eats" is the conjugated form of *to eat*.

5. **Direct Object**: a word or phrase in a sentence referring to the person or thing receiving the action of the verb. In the phrase, "Ed throws the ball to Ned," "ball" is the direct object.

6. **Indirect Object**: the person or thing "to whom" or "for whom" something occurs. In the phrase, "Ed throws the ball to Ned," "Ned" is the indirect object. In the sentence, "She buys the house for Anton," the indirect object is "Anton."

7. **Infinitive (form)**: a name for the verb before it is conjugated. Infinitives always start with "to." For example, "to run," "to study," and "to speak" are all verbs in the infinive form. In Spanish, infinitives end in -ar, -er, -ir (or -se if the verb is reflexive).

8. **Noun**: A word that is used for a name, person, place, thing, quality, or action, and can function as the subject or object of a verb. In the phrase, "Tim runs fast," "Tim" is the noun. In the sentence, "Waves pound the coast," both "waves" and "coast" are nouns.

9. **Pronoun**: the part of speech that substitutes for a noun or noun phrase. The words, *I, you, he, she, we, they, it, them,* etc. are all pronouns.

10. **Verb**: the "action" word in a sentence. The verb can also express existence, or occurrence. In the phrase, "The pilot flies the plane," "flies" is the verb. In the sentence, "She is here," "is" is the verb.

10835241R00103

Made in the USA
Charleston, SC
09 January 2012